Freeing
the Creative Spirit

Drawing on the Power of Art
to Tap the Magic and Wisdom Within

ADRIANA DIAZ

HarperSanFrancisco
A Division of HarperCollins*Publishers*

Grateful acknowledgment is made for permission to reprint excerpts from the following works:

Reprinted from: *Meditations with Hildegard of Bingen* by Gabriele Uhlein. Copyright © 1983 Bear & Co. Inc., by permission of Bear & Co. Inc., P.O. Drawer 2860, Santa Fe, NM 87504. *Meditations with Meister Eckhart*, edited by Matthew Fox. Copyright © 1983 Bear & Co. Inc., by permission of Bear & Co. *A Painter's Quest*, text and illustrations by Peter Rogers. Copyright © 1987, 1988 Peter Rogers by permission of Bear & Co. Inc. "The Panther" from *The Selected Poems of Rainer Maria Rilke*, translated by Robert Bly. Copyright © 1981 by Robert Bly. Reprinted by permission of HarperCollins Publishers. From *The Paintings of Henry Miller: Paint As You Like and Die Happy*, by Henry Miller. Copyright © 1973, published by Chronicle Books. From *The Awakened Eye* by Frederick Franck. Copyright © 1979 by Frederick Franck. Reprinted by permission of Alfred A. Knopf, Inc. Dylan Thomas: *Poems of Dylan Thomas*. Copyright © 1945 by the Trustees for the Copyrights of Dylan Thomas. Reprinted by permission of New Directions Publishing Corporation. The lines from Poem XV (*Twenty-One Love Poems*) from *The Dream of a Common Language, Poems 1974–1977*, by Adrienne Rich, are reprinted by permission of the author and W. W. Norton & Company, Inc. Copyright © 1978 by W. W. Norton & Company, Inc.

FIRST EDITION

Library of Congress Cataloging-in-Publication Data

Diaz, Adriana.
    Freeing the creative spirit : drawing on the power of art to tap
the magic and wisdom within / Adriana Diaz. — 1st ed.
      p.   cm.
    Includes bibliographical references.
    ISBN 0-06-250182-8 (alk. paper)
    1. Spiritual life.   2. Creative ability—Religious aspects.
3. Creation (Literary, artistic, etc.)   4. Art—Psychology.
5. Self. I. Title.
BL624.D38   1992
291.4'46—dc20
                                      90–55771
                                        CIP

94 95 96 VICKS 10 9 8 7 6 5 4 3

This edition is printed on acid-free paper
that meets the American National Standards Institute Z39.48 Standard.

For my father,
who taught me reverent curiosity,
the value of hard work,
personal integrity,
and appreciation for the magic
and wonder of the universe.

Contents

List of Exercises

Foreword

THIS IS A wonderful, rare book for enhancing creativity. Adriana Diaz takes hold of this slippery subject, so full of riddles and subtleties, both by head and tail and by the whole body: the heart, the senses, the capacity for consciousness, and myths—ancestral, personal, social, universal. This exceptional book is part handbook—a detailed and original how-to manual—and part prayer book, meditation primer, spiritual guidebook. Diaz guides us step by step not only to the appropriate moods for working creatively, but leads us to the unfolding of potential and healing of old wounds, especially the wounds of self-belittling and negative self-image, the patterns that are obstacles to letting go and letting be, to play and discovery.

Diaz's thorough commitment to her subject appeals to me tremendously. She knows what she is talking about; she has been there. She is not selling a product, she is eliciting responsiveness and awakening perception. She not only enthusiastically encourages creativity, but also offers specific exercises that lead from one stage to the next. She not only inspires, she is grounded in the procedures that put us at our ease.

"Drawing and painting require mental and spiritual preparation," writes Diaz. Her Creative Meditation process begins with meditation on our divine core; the creative source. She then takes us through a series of ancestral, personal, social, and universal orbits, teaching us to release our resources, express gratitude through ritual and celebration, and prepare ourselves for the revelations of creativity through meditative reverence. This reverence is never abstract, but always enacted by creating a sacred space where awe and delight can safely live. Diaz emphasizes that drawing and painting need our wholeness, body and soul—not perfect, but authentic. Real. Who we are. Yes. Paint that. Look at that leaf. Draw that.

"This type of seeing is an intentional personal engagement. It is an act of spiritual intimacy, a more profound interaction with the world than most of us have ever known. Learning to see and to know communion with creatures, things, and other people can liberate us from the imprisonment of alienation on a personal and global level. When we see ourselves as separate creatures fighting for survival, we devour animals, trees, water, even space without concern or awareness of our effect. The experience of drawing meditation suddenly awakens the eye and the mind to the sacred vitality of the Earth and our connection to all its life forms. This is a truly transformative and sacred experience, and I would encourage those of you who have children to involve the whole family in this meditation practice once you are comfortable with it on your own."

Seeing with the reverential eye, the painter's eye, can guide our planet into an innovative and compassionate future. Shared Creative Meditation leads to trust, is what is needed to make the world community a primary support for the creativity of all people. Diaz's unique and multi-ethnic approach celebrates the rich diversity of world traditions.

From my own intense experience of painting, I know how color can bring one to a magical moment of transcendence. And ordinary consciousness dissolves into a new becoming. We receive this gift through our senses: the energy of the brush stroke, the flow of the paint, the sound of the surface. The power in the small and the concrete makes visible the spirit.

How to justify spending one's time painting in a world filled with so much suffering? The answer is quick on our tongue. The images we receive onto our canvases may have the compassion and radiant truth that will quench society's thirst. Diaz says the artist gives birth to society's images. These images are "the collective host from which the human spirit takes sustenance, nurturance, and hope." No wonder she stresses the necessity of being faithful to the preparation with "prayerful and ceremonial elements."

Freeing the Creative Spirit helps us shed old lies and terrors and masks. It offers a vision that is connected to a cosmic creative flow. Even the most playful exercises carry the spirit of challenge, enlightenment, and joyful participation. In the Breath of God exercise, we move bright colored inks around on a white page by blowing through a straw little pools of color. This improvisation frees us from all illusion of control and grounds us in the certainty of imagination, as we follow the emerging dance.

We are in a New Renaissance, Diaz writes. There is no longer a pat answer to what "real art" looks like. "Art is about integrity and authenticity.

It is about reverence, justice, and dignity." The eye is an organ of the soul; talking about creativity is talking about wholeness and cosmos and deep ecology and creation spirituality and our personal offering to the communion of the world.

This book can be immensely helpful to teachers in the arts, and to individuals trying to find their way to their creative energy. There is generous help as well with questions about art supplies and technical procedures. The book is also relevant to people in small groups who want to share rituals and exercises and need help sharing their experiences.

"Art," Diaz writes, "is a place where daring and caring come together." Her book is such a place. Both qualities are uniquely impressive here, and they inject compassion and vitality into the bloodstream of the reader. One feels the personal presence of the author, always there, encouraging, supporting, explaining, teaching . . . enjoying, delighting in our creative awakening.

This book is a feast: so much information, so much soul stroking, boundless enthusiasm and patience, support for fear and terrors, challenges to our creative readiness, inspiring insights, and a philosophy of creativity that makes it the ultimate ground of our being. Diaz integrates art and the social and ecological redemption of humanity. She demonstrates how learning to see and being willing to feel are preparations for justice making, thus bringing into wholeness the aesthetic and the ethical and freeing the creative spirit to bestow its gifts.

—M. C. RICHARDS

Preface

EVERY BOOK IS an open letter to the world. This one is the culmination of the first half of my intellectual and spiritual life. The route to my current philosophy has taken me through the jungles of religious thought, the forests of psychological theories, the deserts of academia, and the oases of artistic practices. I have stopped only long enough to write this epistle before continuing on my way, for this creative spirit is always curious and ready for the unfolding of the next mystery, the challenges of the next white canvas.

The ideas in this book offer a particular spiritual and psychological perspective. Many of my readers will hear echoes of Meister Eckhart, C. G. Jung, the voices of Buddhism, Western mystics, and favorite poets. These have all been my mentors, and from them I have formulated a process of creative practice that enriches my life and that has brought joy to others. Creative Meditation is a form of aesthetic spiritual expression that I hope will continue to empower people long after my journey's end.

A Word About Language

Two significant linguistic challenges presented themselves in the presentation of this work. The first was the issue of reclaiming words and terminologies that have had traditional religious connotations; the second was the issue of sexist language.

I do not intend Creative Meditation to replace any existing religious practice. I have done my best to honor the deepest meanings of spiritually expressive words, respecting their use as defined by certain religions, while embracing them in a more universal way to accommodate the multicultural perspective of my philosophy.

I have also consciously attempted to make the language in this book as inclusive and nonsexist as possible. Some of the sources cited, however, may not exhibit the same sensitivity to this issue. It is my hope that my sisters (for whenever language is noninclusive it is always women who must adjust to accept the vocabulary) will recognize that each source was selected because it made a significant contribution to the work as a whole.

It is my great hope that everyone who engages with this work will feel respected and welcomed to the playful and prayerful world of painting and drawing.

—ADRIANA DIAZ
Oakland, California

Acknowledgments

THE TASK OF making dreams come true far exceeds wishing upon a star.

Years of dedication to creative work and play have gone into the development of the Creative Meditation process, and finally the reality of this book. Though I have been at the hub of this work, the energy it generates comes from those who have taken part in it and those who have been steadfast supporters: students, friends, and colleagues.

First I want to acknowledge two women without whose vision and love I might never have accomplished any of this work. My deepest appreciation goes to JoAnn McAllister for hours of pouring her considerable intellectual and literary skills over this manuscript, for being an exacting and loving critic and always a supportive friend; and to Jean Searles for years of trust, encouragement, and unfaltering friendship. I wish to thank my mother, Antenette Diaz, for the support and care packages with which she has so lovingly sustained me, and Nancy Carleton for helping me through my fawnlike beginning as a professional writer.

I am fortunate to be a part of a unique and talented professional community. To my friend and colleague Matthew Fox I extend my thanks for the opportunity to teach at the Institute for Culture and Creation Spirituality, and for his courageous dedication to the vision of a world governed by compassion and justice. Thanks to all my colleagues at ICCS, especially Marlene, Robert, and Jim, and to the students who have nurtured my work through their creative risk taking and playfulness.

Special thanks to M. C. Richards for being an ongoing inspiration and role model whose support and friendship I have come to cherish greatly. To Anne, Gerry, Michael, Rhoda, Rusty, Caroline, and Albert my thanks for the shoulders, ears, and hands they were so willing to lend. To Malcolm, thanks for the on-call computer advice.

Finally, an acknowledgment of someone who affected my life many years ago. Guy Emanuele was my high school counselor. He believed I could accomplish something with my life. When others counseled me to "get a nice little job," he encouraged me to take a college entrance exam. Without visible role models I was on the verge of succumbing to the gender and racial stereotypes telling me that Hispanic women did not become educated professionals. I have waited many years to express my gratitude to Guy Emanuele, I hope this book and my years of teaching will be received as a fitting gesture.

Introduction

The Journey of the Creative Spirit

i WAS TAUGHT THAT prayer, like good manners, consisted of "Please" and "Thank you." My religious education had no connection to the many hours I spent coloring, drawing, and painting, which came under the category of "keeping myself entertained." By the time I entered graduate school it became clear that I had made a life's work out of "keeping myself entertained," and through my studies in culture and spirituality I realized that painting and drawing had been and continue to be my deepest expression of gratitude and reverence for the awesome mysteries of life.

One of the earliest spiritual, one might say mystical, experiences of my creative development occurred when, as a young undergraduate art student, I was learning to draw. That experience made me realize that there is more to the world than what seems apparent. We can't usually see the microscopic world or the telescopic world, nor the atomic, subatomic, or nonatomic world, but with a reverential eye we can see beyond the surface of things.

The drawing class was teaching me to develop my eyes to see the things I normally took for granted. I was amazed to realize that I had hardly seen a thing in eighteen years. In class we were looking at the shapes of shadows, the shapes of the spaces between leaves, the surface quality on the edges of objects. This new seeing was awakening me to the world as if it were an entirely new place, and despite the joy of the experience I would leave drawing class exhausted. The end of class usually meant a reversion to my "regular" vision, which meant my eyes were at rest.

One morning, however, my eyes didn't go back to their old pattern. Instead, the sight I was cultivating stayed with me, and as I left the art building and crossed the patio on my usual route to science class, I was literally stopped in my tracks. Every boulder, every leaf, every wooden bench seemed to be speaking to me.

I can only say that I felt as if each thing were revealing itself and calling out to me. Yes, calling out. There was a sound attached to this phenomenon, similar to the deafening sound of crickets and grasshoppers. The air, the light, the objects, even my own body seemed porous and exposed. A window to another dimension of life had opened to me. I felt stunned at first, then privileged, as if I'd been allowed into another realm of the universe.

The experience lasted about two days, then the "window" closed. Some years later I experienced the same thing again, but only for a few hours. I cannot explain this phenomenon in any scientific way; I am not a scientist. Frankly, I don't need any explanations; I simply experienced the incredible shimmering life that is usually invisible to us. This remains a cherished, life-changing event that has been an ongoing inspiration in my life and work.

While I cannot promise that Creative Meditation will give anyone such an experience, I can say that this book and the process it offers are designed to awaken the creative spirit within each person who is willing to devote a little time to the process. Creative Meditation offers deep personal renewal and a joyful sense of self-esteem. It promotes recognition of our human connection to the universe and the divine life force that is our essence. Creative Meditation is a process of freeing the flow of creativity in individuals as well as society.

This is an expressive spiritual practice based on the belief that creativity is a sacred universal energy, a manifestation of the divine. While the human concept of God has taken many forms, one aspect of divinity connects creeds and practices around the world: that of God as supreme creator. In this regard it is natural to recognize that we are most divinely inspired when we exercise our creative impulses and display our passionate emotions, for those are the earthly energies that stimulate transformation, manifest self-expression, and create global change.

Creativity is a combination of making something happen and letting something happen, so Creative Meditation has two stages, one quiet and still, the other spontaneously active and dynamic. Painting, drawing, and mixed media exercises are combined with periods of meditation, reflection, and ritual. While it is an excellent introduction to the joyful rewards of artistic expression, it remains grounded in the spiritual experience of creativity. Creative Meditation is not product oriented; it is designed to free the painter from a preoccupation with the final outcome. The result of this freedom is a more rewarding and self-affirming creative experience. The skills and techniques of drawing and painting develop along the way, and the relaxation meditations release the body's energy, allowing it to flow. Creative Meditation is a prayerful integration of play, self-discovery, community building, and aesthetic spirituality.

Talent: Tradition, Myth, and Reality

I must confess to being a bit of an agnostic when it comes to a belief in talent. Talent is a product-oriented word. It has no connection to the depth of human experience inherent in the creative act. The term is so charged that whether people believe they have it or not, the label traps everyone in a cage of expectations. Those expectations ("I can't do anything" or "I must do something") alienate people from the spontaneous joy of the process.

While I agree that certain individuals possess the right body for gymnastics, can instinctively identify middle C, or have a natural ability to create a likeness with a pencil, I believe that these predispositions are only a starting point. It is too easy to think of talent as some kind of divine dowry bestowed on certain people that makes them better than everyone else.

If talent is to be a factor in the success of any person, it must be combined with discipline, tenacity, relentless dedication, and the ability to sacrifice the ego for the sake of the process. I have known many people who use talent as an excuse for not trying. If you are either hiding behind the "T" word or using it as a shield, it's time to assess this issue in a realistic way so that you can have some fun and stand up with dignity for your own creative potential. Honor your desire and your right to devote whatever time you need to your self-expression.

The creation of art as a professional activity and academic discipline, the development of museums, galleries and concert halls, and the narrow methodology of teaching the arts to young children have intimidated people into thinking that art is an activity of the educated, the sophisticated, the credentialed. Art making as a playful, life-supporting activity thus becomes the province of the professionals.

JOSEPH ZINKER

Exercise: Reflection #1

The following questions are designed to help you assess your belief and assumptions about your own creative potential while developing an understanding of your personal evolution. Don't try to answer them quickly in one sitting. Carry the questions in your mind for a few days before writing the answers. After finishing a few of the projects return to them to reconsider your answers. You may have gained new important insights through the creative process.

➤Do I live with a personal myth about my talent? If so, what is it and where did it come from?

➤Am I living with someone else's expectations? What kind of an effect is this having on me?

➤Of my personal acquaintances and family members, whom do I consider to be talented? Why do I think this of them? What is their talent? Do I know the story of their development, or do I assume that they've had none? (I suggest that you talk with these people about their talent.)

➤What talents do I possess? What do other people consider to be my talents? (Don't be afraid to ask.)

The fundamentally unique aspect of Creative Meditation as an art education approach is that it rests upon a conscious recognition of creativity as sacred activity, a process of spiritual engagement that I define as a profound human awareness of deep connection to a universal life force. This sense of spiritual engagement is present to a certain degree whenever a person is called to create, but it is seldom addressed in traditional art education, and it is especially omitted from basic introductory courses that would reach a broad range of students. As a result, drawing and painting are left to "the talented ones" (who are really the determined ones), and too many people walk through life with a sense of failure and lack of self-respect where creativity is concerned.

Creative Meditation is a means toward a more spiritual creativity and a more creative spirituality. It can become a spiritual practice for those who have no other, or it can become an adjunct to an already established discipline. Experiencing creative activity as dynamic prayer frees the pro-

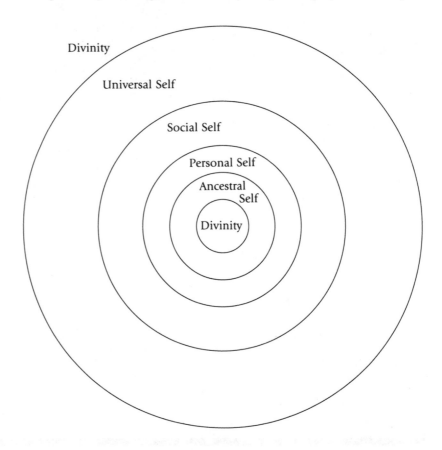

cess from the expectations enmeshed in the term *art*. Success in the Creative Meditation process is measured by pleasure, aesthetic engagement, spiritual wholeness, and a sense of self-esteem.

The diagram provided is a visual tool for understanding the basic philosophy behind Creative Meditation. By studying it and the succeeding explanation you will have laid the groundwork for starting our work together. Beginning in chapter 1 we will proceed out from the core of divinity, exploring the realms of the ancestral, personal, social, and universal selves through creative experiences, rituals, meditations, and reflective questions.

Think of this series of concentric circles as a spiritual cross-section of human life. This life is a membrane through which the creative energy of the divine flows freely. As you can see, the rings surround and are surrounded by divinity. Creative Meditation presumes a core of divinity within each person.

The first ring, the *ancestral self*, is the evolutionary legacy of our species. Each person carries a genetic inheritance. This is both a species inheritance and a personal genetic inheritance. The DNA and other evolutionary developments with which we are born carry on and procreate *Homo sapiens sapiens*. At the same time we are the current representatives of familial and racial ancestors whose passions brought us into being. Deep in our flesh and bones resides a constant and reliable source of encouragement from these ancestors, which I call *inherent affirmation*.

Inherent affirmation is a key element in the restoration of personal creativity. It grows from the knowledge that our very existence is the culmination of millions of years of preparation. Millions of years of evolution have prepared us for creative activity. The development of the human hand and voluntary muscle coordination allow us to hold and manipulate a brush, see colors, take a deep breath, and decide spontaneously how we will apply paint to a surface. Millions of life forms stand behind us as the physical firmament upon which we stand. I accept as my ancestor every life form which has contributed to the development of the human body I possess. I can only imagine that if they could speak, they would express a hope that their lives have contributed to something wonderful. All of life supports our best effort and is rooting for our success. This is inherent affirmation of every positive step we take.

By going deep into the nature of human evolution, Creative Meditation recognizes that creativity is a natural characteristic of our species. That which is ancient is also newly born in each of us. Meditating on our divine core and our ancestral self can nurture trust and self-respect. Painting, drawing, and play are means of celebrating our physical and mental gifts.

To understand the *personal self,* think back to how you came to know yourself. Little by little we awaken to consciousness, and as we grow, we develop greater powers of self-reflection. Long before we know the word *ego* we have one, and by the time we are adults we recognize that we consist of things we know about ourselves as well as a treasury of mysteries. We credit Sigmund Freud with the invention of psychology, but the exploration of the personal self has been on the human agenda for centuries. The personal self is all you know yourself to be, conscious and unconscious. It is an ever-expanding source of images, understanding, and wonder. It is your inner face as well as the interface with which you meet the world. In Creative Meditation the personal self reaps the rewards of greater awareness through reflection, play, and creative risk taking.

The human is a social animal, and as the personal self moves beyond the realm of inner involvement another dimension of the self emerges from within a communal context. This is the *social self.* It encompasses interpersonal relationships from partnership and family to the larger social context of community membership, political affiliation, and citizenship. Certain aspects of the personal self are visible only within social contexts.

Finally we come to the *universal self,* the suprapersonal level of existence. To understand the universal self, I ask you to accept the paradox of being a space that is not actually you, but a space contained by the physical being that you are. The universal self is the space we contain. It is not connected to ego or personal controls. Since we are eventually most in our universal self when we're dead, let's look at this ring from that perspective. We usually think about the body decomposing as if it became nothing, but it doesn't become nothing. The body eventually yields to the spaces within and around it. The cavities become bigger, as solid matter yields to natural atomic transformation. We return to the elements from which we were born. In death the body yields to a more spacious existence, becoming once again an integral part of the nonhuman universe. Our atomic structure is reassembled, and we seem to disappear.

At the beginning of this discussion I asked you to think of life as a membrane through which divine creative energy flows. The divinity at our core is the inner dynamic manifestation of the Infinite Divine, which is the source of all creative force. Humans, indeed all life forms, are the membrane through which divine energy pulsates.

In ancient cultures art was the mediator between the human and the world of divine mystery into which consciousness was born. Before the role of priest was relegated to certain individuals, the prayerful power of creativity, whether expressed through dance, chanting, mask making, or painting, was recognized as a personal responsibility. In primal cultures

Creativity is a different quality of spiritual life than humility and asceticism; it is the revelation of the god-like nature of humanity.
NICHOLAS BERDYAEV

the arts are still essential means of interaction with the divine, and the artifacts created in the service of worship retain an especially powerful presence regardless of their age or condition. There still exist contemporary forms of ancient artistic spiritual traditions. The Japanese art of Sumi painting, for example, is a prayerful practice. Navajo sand painting is a sacred act in direct communion with the earth. In India, colored flower petals and powders are laid out in intricate designs on the ground, in doorways, and along holy processional routes. Dervishes have spinning prayer, and Africans drum and dance. Chanting, meditation, the burning of incense, prostration—all these activities are dynamic forms of prayer. It is the aim of Creative Meditation to add a consciously spiritual dimension to Euro-centered practices of artistic expression.

Ceremony and Ritual

Unlike our Eastern brothers and sisters, we contemporary Westerners are largely unaccustomed to rituals or ceremonies as part of daily life. Nevertheless, ceremony has developed as an important part of the Creative Meditation process. Such practices may seem awkward or strange at first, but it's important to do some form of the ceremonies prepared. The directions have been clearly and simply laid out step by step, and in resource 4 you'll find guidelines to help you develop ceremonies with others. If, by the end of the book, extensive personal rituals have not gained importance for you as an ongoing practice, simplify this dimension of the Creative Meditation practice. I suggest candle or incense lighting as a minimum practice. This small ritual gives you a moment to close your eyes, center, and sink into a calm and quiet place. It allows time to remember that you are not creating in order to produce a product, and that you are one of the mysteries of the universe continually unfolding and revealing itself out of darkness.

"Dabbling"

Without a concern for the spiritual integrity and depth of personal encounter that accompanies self-expression, too many crafts and creative activities have been traditionally taught as "hobby art," product-oriented pastimes. While this approach may satisfy the needs of some, it misses the most enriching aspect of creative activity: transformation and growth. As a result, the participants tend to diminish their work, seeing it as "dabbling" or "playing around." I hate to hear people dismiss and devalue their efforts this way. Dabbling suggests superficiality, lack of intent, and lack of importance. In Creative Meditation there's no such thing as dabbling, because every aspect of the creative process is honorable and intentional. Play, chaos, delight, confusion all have a place alongside prayer in creativity and in life.

In Creative Meditation the spiritual experience of creativity is seen as the foundation of all art-related activities. Focusing on the meditative aspect of creativity frees up "the instrument," which is the whole person. Until the whole person is free, nothing can be achieved. Just as muscles must be warmed up and conditioned before athletic activity, so the psyche and spirit of a person must be conditioned and supple before creativity can flow freely.

Getting to the Real Magic

Creativity is the real magic of our universe. It is the shape of our courage and the force of our souls. Creativity is the matrimonial language of form and space, consummated in the physical and spiritual expressions of humanity.

This book has been created with a great deal of care, affection, and pride as a challenging gift to those who are ready to acknowledge the pregnant darkness within. It is designed to be a companion and a catalyst. I hope that each copy becomes worn and dog-eared, lined and notated. Spaces have been designed for notes and reflections, as an invitation to create a personalized copy, a communion of our creative energies. I feel, in a very symbolic sense, like the archetypal fairy godmother here to remind you that the real magic is inside of you. May this book spark and nurture your unique and prolific creativity.

Exercise: The Signature—
A Declaration of Creative Selfhood

You have been given a place on the opening page of this book to sign your name. More than an invitation to state ownership, this is the first exercise in self-discovery. If you haven't already signed your name in the place provided, please do so now.

If you could collect samples of your signature throughout your life, as an archaeologist collects artifacts from ancient civilizations, you would see evidence of your own evolution. We human beings seem to have a natural tendency toward self-naming as a means of self-definition. Throughout life our signature not only identifies the person we are, it also is our most intimate and unique form of self-expression. As art is a manifestation of a collective story, a means of cultural identity, the art of an era is the signature of its people. Just so, your signature tells your story, not in the name itself, but in the way you express it: the size of it, the slant, the quality of the line.

Exploring the Signature

Your signature is your primary self-expression. It is something you create every day. No one, not even the finest forgery expert, can create it exactly the way you do. It lives in the muscle memory of your body where your arm, hand, shoulders, and back retain a certain pattern for creating your signature. Any restriction of those muscles and bones limits the full expression of that pattern.

Here's a suggestion for exploring those body movements further:

➤Tape some large plain paper onto a smooth wall (newsprint or butcher paper are best).

➤Sign your name very large, feeling the pronounced movements of your body, especially in the shoulders and back.

➤Re-create your signature at various speeds and sizes, with a continuing awareness of your body.

➤After you have signed with your dominant hand, try it with your nondominant hand.

➤When you're finished, turn the signature page upside down. In this direction it loses the instantaneous ego identification. Look at the line quality of your name. Is the line smooth? Angular? Tense? What is your response to it? Are you passing judgment on it or on yourself? Treat it as if it were a piece of art. Look at its placement on the page, its size, and the slope of the letters. Was it difficult to make it big?

➤If you are criticizing or judging yourself for the way you did this exercise, or the look of your signature, let this be your first step toward self-acceptance.

Write down the message your critical voice is giving you. (You might want to invest in some unlined typing paper: this voice can be long-winded!) Keep writing until it has exhausted itself.

Now write the rebuttal to that voice. This is your signature. It is meant to be exactly the way you sign it. It can't be wrong. If your muscles are tight and the name seems constricted, then this has simply been a lesson from your body. It's time to stretch.

When you have finished writing the rebuttal, sign it.

This is an exercise you can do whenever you hear that judgmental voice. Often, putting the critical words in writing releases the energy and power that builds up inside. Eventually you'll see how absurd the critic is, and how he or she is never satisfied with anything. Remember: your personal approach is valid and creative. While there may be easier or quicker ways to do certain things, there's no totally wrong way to do the exercises in this book. Just relax and let your creative energy flow.

The Painting Journal

Essential to Creative Meditation and the process introduced in this book is a painting journal: an unlined sketchbook devoted to colors, images, lines, and textures. This can also become a nest for newborn poetry or creative reflection, but it should not be the same book you use as a daily written journal. Our reliance on language (which is a linear form) so dominates our other powers of perception (spatial, intuitive, optical) that it is easy to lose sight of the purpose of a journal devoted primarily to the exploration of images and nonverbal expression.

The painting journal is a tool of synthesis, a contemplative space where life and art can combine in spontaneous expression. While the projects explained in each chapter will take special time to do, the painting journal can go with you at any time. I suggest a six-by-nine-inch spiral bound book that will fit into a backpack, basket, or glove compartment. I have found that anything much larger is cumbersome to carry and awkward to keep close at hand. Remember, this is not the paper you will use for the projects described in the book. While I may make suggestions regarding meditative projects to be done in the journal, it is a separate, ongoing work space where you are free to stretch the ideas and images that begin with the designed projects. You will find, as you read further, that I presume you are using such a journal as an accompaniment to the directed process.

Keep the journal with you as much as possible. I take mine to the movies and sketch in the dark; it's fun to see what's on the page when I get home. I often develop those images or ideas at a later date in the light. I hope that you will continue with the journal even after you have finished doing the projects in this book. My journals have become such an important resource that I number the pages and date each entry for easy reference.

All the black and white line drawings in the text of this book have come from my journals.

Above all, remember that the journal is your workshop/playshop. You may tear out any entries, scribble, glue, shred, and so on. These are all part of the creative process.

It's easy to grow flowers
above ground,
Sun does all the work.
What beauty, friend,
grows in your darkness?
What hothouse, earthen-
*   ware gift*
do you bring today?

How to
Use This Book

CREATIVE MEDITATION PROJECTS are designed to be instructional as well as enlightening. Whether you do them alone or with a group, you'll be challenged in a number of ways. Ultimately, the entire process is designed for the enrichment of your life, so you can expect it to evoke new things. You'll have moments of great accomplishment and moments of frustration. You'll have days when wonderful things seem to magically drip off your brush, and other days when nothing goes right.

Everyone, even the professional artist, has such ups and downs. Don't take yourself too seriously, and don't make creativity a job. If you're feeling tied in knots, set your work aside. There are enough situations in life that produce anxiety and self-criticism, Creative Meditation should not become one of them.

Guidelines

Below are some guidelines to facilitate your creative process and your use of this book. These are important reminders to turn to whenever you have a problem or feel stuck. It might be helpful to read back through them from time to time just for support.

➤*Be gentle and patient with yourself.* You're learning to develop a creative process. Not everyone does this process the same way. Go at your own pace.

It may take some time to learn the natural rhythms of your body, the order in which you feel comfortable doing things, and the place in which you like to work. Learn to give yourself the patience and support that no one else has given you.

➤*Let go of the end product.* "Impossible!" you say. I suggest this as a guideline, knowing very well how difficult it is. Working with a finished product in mind can be counterproductive for anyone, for someone beginning a creative pursuit it can be paralyzing.

➤*Surrender to the paint and the process.* This is the only thing that will help free you from the finished-product syndrome. Please believe me when I tell you that this surrender is essential to every person in the arts regardless of fame or success. If you don't surrender to the materials, the images, and the process, your painting will become contrived and manipulated. Just as dreams take place without conscious intervention or manipulation, paintings will flow out of you the more you learn to trust the process.

➤*Always begin painting or drawing with a brief meditation or ceremony.* These can help center and calm a frazzled mind and spirit. Use the rituals and ceremonies provided, or use the guidelines in resource 4 at the end of this book to design personal rituals for focusing your energies. If some unidentifiable thing is bothering you as you get started, use a ritual or meditation to get to the root of it. These can also help you let go of the product idea.

➤*Keep the painting journal, and always have it at hand.* Please see the section on the painting journal for more specific information. This journal is a very important part of the Creative Meditation approach.

➤*Always read through all the directions before beginning any exercise or project.*

➤*Use the resources and Bibliography for help.* If the supplies segment of resource 1 does not sufficiently answer your questions about media or tools, for instance, check the Bibliography, which lists several excellent resource books.

➤*Become acquainted with your local art supply store.* Take yourself on a "field trip" to become acquainted with the assortment of materials available. You may feel overwhelmed at first, but take this book with you and focus on the supplies you'll need for the first couple of chapters. Start out simply. The first two exercises don't even require a brush. To begin, buy finger paints and finger-paint paper, a few brilliant watercolors or colored inks, and some sturdy all-purpose paper. You'll also need a painting journal.

Art store salespeople are usually very helpful. They're usually artists or art students. Get to know one or two specific people so that you can ask their advice by phone if need be.

To paint is to love again, and to love is to live to the fullest. . . . To live and love, and to give expression to it in paint, one must also be a true believer. There must be something to worship. Where in this broad land is the holy of holies hidden?
HENRY MILLER

One necessary limitation we must place on ourselves is that of restraining ourselves, through self-discipline, from expecting quick results. Our inferiors impatiently measure the other person's behavior to see if we are having an effect. The I Ching explains that we must learn to work with time as the vehicle of the Creative Force. Working with time, adapting to the fact that slow progress is the only progress that endures, is part of the process of non-action. We need to withdraw from impatience and "flow," as with water that only runs downhill.

CAROL ANTONY

➤ *Develop a work area.* This should be your designated space. Ask housemates or family to respect that your supplies and work remain private. You should be able to leave works in progress somewhere to dry knowing that they won't be looked at if you don't want them to be. Your work area should also house your supplies. If you don't have shelves or drawers, set up a private grocery box. I highly recommend cleaning the work space as little as possible. Learn to think of clutter and dust in a new way. Try to realize that dirt in your house is simply displaced from outside. You can choose just what you'd like to do with it. You can collect it, throw it out, or use it as an art medium! (Seriously.)

➤ *Vary work spaces and places.* Sometimes a change of scene can alter your creative process. Try it out. The projects can be done over and over again in a multitude of settings. Drawing meditation can be done alone in silence or at the park, where the music of the universe consists of squealing children and barking dogs chasing Frisbees. Your subject and your process will be very different.

➤ *Follow the order of presentation.* While it's not absolutely necessary that you do all the exercises in the exact order in which they appear, they are presented in this order for your maximum benefit. Do them as many times as you like, and by the time you've gone through the book taking the projects and exercises in order, you'll no doubt have developed favorite exercises, media, or processes. The painting journal is a great place for concentrated exploration.

➤ *Be open to spontaneity, making things up as you go along.* I have tried to be as explicit as possible in giving directions and supplying information to facilitate the process for those who are completely unfamiliar with drawing and painting. If you are such a person, please realize also that I encourage exploration with tools as much as the exploration of images. As you develop your collection of supplies, try many sizes of brushes and grades of pencils.

➤ *Experiment with materials and tools, traditional and nontraditional.* Be creative with unorthodox implements. For example, try drawing with the burned ends of twigs, or dip them in ink. Imprint images or patterns with rocks, shells, kitchen utensils, or found objects.

➤ *Try to incorporate Creative Meditation practice into your daily life.* If you're feeling frightened or nervous, for example, be creatively nervous. Get out the journal and make nervous marks or put down the colors of your fear. Whether you're happy or depressed, angry, or in love, find out the colors and shapes of your emotions.

➤*Be ready and willing to make a mess.* Give yourself permission to get your hands dirty or to drip on the floor. Plastic drop cloths used for house painting are cheap, and quick to fold up. Needless to say, you'll probably want an apron.

➤*Get used to chaos in your head.* In the creative process one must surrender to possibility. This means letting go of concrete plans and organized ideas.

The degree to which you invite chaos into your space is up to you. Some artists, like the great contemporary English painter Francis Bacon, thrive on chaotic surroundings. Photos of Bacon's studio show that it is so cluttered he seemed hardly able to reach the canvas. He applied dust and dirt to his paintings with a rag to enhance surface quality and texture. In Bacon's case, the chaos is eventually resolved into well-organized paintings that are exquisitely painted with a brilliant use of color.

➤*Use a portable tape player.* A cassette player is an integral part of most instructions. It's useful for playing music, of course, but there will also be times when you might want to talk aloud about what you're doing, or about the subject of your work.

➤*Use the Bibliography as an ongoing resource.* The Bibliography is an excellent listing of books related to creativity, art, and the sacred. I highly recommend that you use this as an extension of what you've begun here.

➤*Save all the work you do as you go along.* This is very important. You may want to throw some things away when you're finished working with the book, but until that time, keep everything you do. Remember that the things you don't like will make the things you do like look even better by contrast. This is the only way you'll be able to see the progress you've made.

➤*Establish a support group.* This isn't always necessary, or possible, but it can be very helpful and a lot of fun. In choosing such a group be selective about your companions. They should be compassionate, supportive, and willing to share their own struggles as well as witnessing yours. You can travel through the book together, working separately but coming together for discussions and sharing work when you like.

Am I willing to give up what I have in order to be what I am not yet? Am I willing to let my ideas of myself, of man be changed? Am I able to follow the spirit of love into the desert? To empty myself even of my concept of emptiness?

M. C. RICHARDS

17

But the artist persists because he has the will to create, and this is the magic power which can transform and transfigure and transpose and which will ultimately be transmitted to others.

ANAÏS NIN

➤*Persevere.* Don't give up. Keep drawing and painting. Each piece is another feather in your cap, a gift you give to yourself in celebration of your creative spirit. You will slowly develop self-confidence, and your reluctance will subside.

➤*Turn barriers into gateways.* While creativity is a free-flowing energy, there are occasions when a person can experience what is popularly called a "creative block." This can be a frightening paralysis of the naturally imaginative and productive mechanisms of the human mind.

The key to overcoming these barriers is in reimaging the phenomenon. Rather than seeing a huge impermeable wall of granite or concrete, I prefer to see the impasse as a locked gate.

In my experience such locked gates have more to do with inner spiritual and psychological development than with paint. Go into yourself to find clues about the hidden key. Pay attention to your dreams, memories, fears, and desires. Until you find what you need, do two things: (1) keep your sense of humor; and (2) keep working. Continuing to paint and draw during such times means getting rid of mistakes and learning from them along the way. Sometimes the key is found in aimless painting and experimentation. Getting rid of the barrier involves letting go of your ego and of the need to control things. The experimentation done at the threshold of a locked gate can not only fill the time with enjoyable hours, it can lead to the very treasure you were looking for.

Filling the mind with positive space is essential to filling life with positive events. Focusing on the accumulation of transgressions or ruminating over past choices keeps you living in the past. Allow painting to be a pleasure and a joy. Get in the habit of saying, "I accept every stroke unconditionally."

➤*Take time for reflections and personal paleontology.* Paleontology is the study of fossils, the remnants of past lives that may have been forgotten or lost under the weight of time. These fossils are actually the foundation upon which the present is built.

The reflection questions are a first step in the process of taking personal inventory. The reflection process provides you with evidence: fossils on the surface and then those lodged in the layers of your whole person. Respond to the questions as honestly as possible, because only you have the answers. Take your time; this process is very important. Your contemplation may dig up memories and information previously forgotten or put away.

Read through all the questions in a reflection segment, then set the book aside and carry the questions in your mind for a while. You may want to do some free writing about each one. (Free writing is nonstop stream-of-consciousness writing. Nothing is censored. Do it for at least five minutes.) If you feel too vulnerable writing your answers in the book, write them in a journal or designate a space in your painting journal for them. If you have developed a support group, you could consider exploring some of the questions there. Discussion can be a terrific catalyst for sparking memories and emotions.

Questions

Here is a list of questions designed to help you reflect on your process whenever you feel stuck or out of touch with a particular project:

➤Am I taking my time with this? Or am I trying to rush through it? Why am I doing this?

➤If I have decided that I don't like this project, what is it that I don't like? Is it demanding too much of me? Is it forcing me to reveal too much of myself?

➤Do I have expectations of myself, or of my work? Do I have a preconceived idea of what this exercise should look like?

➤Am I hearing some critical voice in my head? Whose voice is it, or where did I learn the things the voice is saying to me?

The Zen of Crumpled Paper

Why was I so impatient since I was already at the place to which I thought I was going?

Affirmations

No doubt you will have some of your own pertinent questions as well, and when you've finished with your reflections, I suggest you light a candle and meditate on the light that shines in you. Write a single-sentence affirmation and remind yourself that creativity requires perseverance. Keep up the good work!

Some examples of affirmations:

➤I am part of the flow of the universe; my expression is a valuable addition to the planet.

➤My work is valuable as an authentic expression of my unique personhood.

➤The relaxation of my body and mind will allow me greater self-expression.

CHAPTER ONE

Reviving
the Ancestral Self

*S*OME OF THE most valuable monuments to human creativity are not to be found in museums or galleries. They are found, instead, on the walls of ancient caves and cliffs around the world. I refer, of course, to the prehistoric paintings of ancestral peoples, which bear witness to the deeply spiritual nature of human creativity. The drawings, paintings, and markings of our ancestors (which they began making thirty thousand years ago) were prayers offered as mediation between the human and the awesome powers of the universe. Evidence suggests that such paintings were part of sacred preparatory and celebratory activities. Hunting is a prime example. The hunt, a life-threatening and life-giving event, was preceded by ritual preparation. Paintings of prey invoked the spirit of the animal and requested that the animal yield its life for the health and nurturance of the tribe.

Cave paintings are evidence that since ancient times the human has recognized not only the power of images but also the power of creating them. Petroglyphs and hieroglyphs have recorded human cultural development. The markings and images of all people are our joint heritage, a heritage that we carry forward every time we pick up a pencil. The creation of images is part of an ancient priesthood handed to us through time from the ancient ones who first drew the bison, and the archetypal images of the ancestors continue to be the expression of our most essential selves.

Reconnecting with the ring of the ancestral self doesn't require a study in anthropology. The ongoing movement to revive racial history and traditions in the United States continues to be essential to the cultivation of creativity, especially within the urban environment. This reawakening of the ancestral ring, which began in the late 1960s and 1970s as part of a conscious movement of reclaiming the pride of ethnic heritage, is responsible for the current abundance of colorful inner-city murals celebrating forgotten stories and little-known

When I became interested . . . in Negro art and I made what they refer to as the Negro Period in my painting, it was because at that time I was against what was called beauty in the museums. At that time, for most people a Negro mask was an ethnographic object. When I went for the first time . . . to the Trocadéro museum . . . I stayed and studied. Men had made those masks and other objects for a sacred purpose as a kind of mediation between themselves and the unknown hostile forces that surrounded them, in order to overcome their fear and horror by giving it a form and an image . . . I realized that this was what painting was all about. Painting isn't an aesthetic operation; it's a form of magic designed as a mediator between this strange, hostile world and us, a way of seizing the power by giving form to our terrors as well as our desires. When I came to that realization, I knew I had found my way.

PABLO PICASSO

heroes and heroines. The music, dance, and literature of minority cultures has become a part of school curricula in many places. This movement has not only brought honor to thousands of people, it has awakened an awareness of world cultures throughout the country.

To achieve this revival of ancestral connection and personal pride, you may want to go back through family photos or heirlooms. Listen to the stories of your elders. We are seldom encouraged to ask our grandparents to tell their stories, and yet their stories are our stories as well.

Creativity is our species' natural response to the challenges of human experience. As our primary power, it remains the mediator between the human soul and the forces beyond our control.

In childhood we are most like those ancestors who gave expression to awe and wonder, because we are neither manipulated nor enculturated beyond our natural responses. By adulthood, however, many of us may have lost most of the wide-eyed wonderment of our childhood. Within the complexities and challenges of adulthood, we reserve our amazement for medical breakthroughs and technological discoveries.

In this chapter we'll begin to unleash our creative energies by doing two things:

1. Recognizing the sacred nature of our creative yearnings, which connect us to the ancestors, and
2. Reviving the natural freedom to play what we enjoyed as children.

We begin with these two basic steps because they return us to our deepest experiences of creative purity. As children we naturally expressed the inherent creative response that our prehistoric ancestors trusted and relied upon into adulthood. As a species we have not lost our organic capacity for creativity, so in order to awaken our creative spirit we must look to the ancestors as our historical role models, and to our own childhood as a teacher.

Play: Creative Autonomy

Creative Meditation is a practice of broadening the aesthetic and spiritual margins of life by freeing the creative spirit, which has been forced to adapt to the rules of authorities and the demands of contemporary life. The most important part of this process is where we will begin: having fun.

The word *fun* may sound a bit frivolous amid talk of sacred ancestors and priesthood, but having fun in this context means restoring the lost enthusiasm and delight of childhood. This fun has a sacred dimension: it is an essential step toward human wholeness. As a part of the Creative Meditation process, fun means warming up your creative muscles and reexperiencing the joy of play.

Recently, while waiting in line at the post office, I watched a young mother at the head of the line busy with her mailing concerns and two young children. The toddler demanded her attention from his stroller while her tiny son, about age four, was content to entertain himself.

He unself-consciously lay on the floor exploring various postures and the capacity of his little limbs to bend and curl. Eventually, he looked up and became fascinated with the ceiling. Flapping legs and arms aimlessly, he occasionally indicated points of interest with his fingers skyward. Over and over he tried communicating to his mother the excitement of his discoveries with exclamations and shouts of delight. Mother, of course, was busy with other responsibilities. Her only response to him was an increasingly vehement command to get up off the floor.

With total compassion for this harried young woman, I asked myself what it would be like if we had not had someone teach us to get up off the floor. The post office line by that time consisted of six to eight adults: middle class, nicely dressed, varying in ages from thirtysomething to seventysomething. I thought about how each person in this line had preserved their innocent curiosity and playfulness somewhere in the recesses of the psyche. I had to contain my laughter when in my mind's eye I imagined us all lying on the floor next to this child flapping arms and legs, sticking out tongues to see how far they could reach, and yelling exuberantly at the top of our voices.

The contrast between my mental image and the reality was striking. Our sedate and composed patience seemed glaring evidence of creative repression. Certainly, many people find outlets to quench their creative thirsts, but few of us manage to recapture the delight of meaningless play.

As you progress through this book you will grow in your ability to be playful, for playfulness is the ultimate form of creative autonomy. It is non-goal-oriented and nonreasonable (this is not the same as unreasonable). Playfulness is whylessness. It is spontaneous celebration and exploration.

Looking at the way in which our understanding of play changes through childhood can help us to reclaim that spontaneous play and learn how to choose between non-goal-oriented play and game play. Our language and culture reflect some misleading ideas about play by an almost synonymous association with games. Using the verb *to play* in conjunction with *game* has led us to believe that when we are involved in a game we are always playing. Competitive games are an interactive experience with

If only human beings could . . . be more reverent toward their own fruitfulness . . . our enjoyment of it is so indescribably beautiful and rich only because it is full of inherited memories of the engendering and birthing of millions.
RAINER MARIA RILKE

predetermined goals, rules, and acceptable means allowed for achieving the desired result.

The play exemplified by the little boy in the post office is pure play. It is full of discovery and wonder; it engages the imagination as well as the intellect in a natural and fun learning process. "Playing" football, tennis, or softball, though it may be fun, is about other things entirely. Competitive situations surround a person with hierarchical political structures, rules, and the intimidating prospect of winning or losing. All these elements work to separate the "players" according to dexterity, intelligence, personality type, and levels of motivation. The concept of a team as a group of people working together toward a common goal can turn into a competition within the competition. Each person not only wants to be acceptable to their peers, but entertains fantasies of becoming the "most valuable player," thereby ensuring the respect and admiration of fellow team members and loved ones.

While competitive play provides some uniquely beneficial lessons for children and adults alike (i.e., camaraderie, tenacity, discipline, mutual support), many children suffer damage to self-image and self-esteem when game play replaces nonrational play. In my experience, men are the most joyful about reclaiming autonomous playfulness because from childhood they have been caught in a world of competition, goal achievement, and the rigors of proving themselves as winners. If nonrational play is not abandoned completely in favor of competitive play, some balance can be achieved. When autonomous play is replaced by structured game playing, fear of failure and humiliation alienate us from our capacity for creative risk taking. The pressures of acceptability and performance anxiety can begin to undermine self-esteem and creative risk taking at a very early age.

Recognizing those factors that have contributed to our development empowers us to name the parts of ourselves that need waking up, and the Creative Meditation process provides the tools for the task. Creative Meditation thrives on free play. This book is about learning (or relearning) how to splash around in the sea of your own imagination.

Creative Meditation and Personal Transformation

To begin reawakening your creative powers by transforming some of the attitudes you have developed about yourself over the years, we're going to focus on two processes: ritual and creative play. Creating and performing

And if we are to believe the ancients, creation is play. Whoever the Creator may be, one feels that He is not concerned with success or failure, sorrow or joy, but with the drama itself. . . . And so it is not the happy ending or the bad ending that matters, but the endless transmutation of which we are witness and prime mover at one and the same time.

HENRY MILLER

rituals or ceremonies does not mean replacing your current religious or spiritual practices with strange, occult activities. If you've never celebrated a personal ritual, I think you'll find this an empowering addition to your life.

Before conducting our first ceremony, it seems fitting to create a place for such an activity. The following altarpiece project combines serious thought about important spiritual questions with a fun cut-and-paste, paint-if-you-like project.

Exercise:
The Triptych Altarpiece

The experience of sacred space makes possible the "founding of the world": where the sacred manifests itself in space, the real unveils itself, the world comes into existence. . . . Every world is the work of the gods, for it was either created directly by the gods or was consecrated, hence cosmicized, by men ritually reactualizing the paradigmatic act of Creation.
—MIRCEA ELIADE*

Our first project creates a place, a sacred space constructed from ordinary supplies and transformed through your unique ideas and desires. I call it the Triptych Altarpiece because I designed the project around that traditional form of religious art found in the great European cathedrals. The historic altarpieces were painted on three separate wooden panels that were hinged together. The two side panels, when closed, presented images that introduced the interior theme, usually the Crucifixion. In this cardboard variation, however, the sides are meant to remain open, though any and all parts of the structure can be painted or decorated. This altarpiece, painted or collaged with personal motifs, can provide a quiet meditation corner that doesn't take up a lot of space. The reflection done during the creative process of this project is a way of connecting the personal self with the core of divinity and the ancestral self. The most important questions to hold in your mind and heart during this project are "What do I believe in?" and "What is sacred to me?"

You can do the project in a day or a week, but don't let it drag along for lack of attention. If you think you might fall into such a pattern, set a completion goal date.

Supplies

* A cardboard box (you determine the size according to space, etc.)
* Possibilities: gesso, paint, assorted found objects, fabric and/or materials for collage
* Scissors or straight-edge blade
* Significant personal objects, which may change seasonally or according to the occasion
* Tape, glue, stapler

---

* Mircea Eliade, *The Sacred and the Profane* (New York: Harcourt Brace Jovanovich, 1959), 64–65.

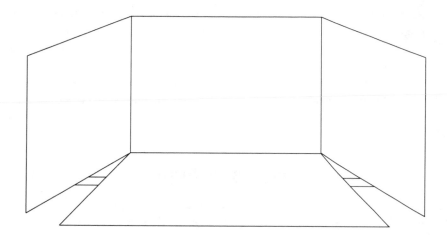

How to Proceed

Let the box sit around the house for a few days (you will cut it later). You might want to sketch some ideas in your painting journal. Live with the questions. Look at the special things in your home: photos, old letters, sea shells, rocks. We call them mementos for lack of a better word. Sometimes we denigrate them by referring to them as dust catchers, because we have never been taught to claim the sacred dimensions of our lives. Those cherished objects can be rotated on the altar, according to seasons or personal celebrations. Let them lead you to the feelings that live inside you. Memorabilia, old photos, and keepsakes are icons of the personally sacred. They are our connections to the ancestors through archetypal experience as well as genetics.

Along with your own sacred objects, you will want symbolic representations of the four elements: water, earth, air, fire. Many Native American cultures have traditionally recognized and welcomed the spirits of the elements at sacred places and ceremonies; this altar project allows us to adopt this practice to enrich our daily lives.

Water. Did you ever realize that in the universe as we know it, water exists nowhere but on Earth? Other planets have vapors or ice, but only Earth contains water in liquid form. Considering the decreasing availability of potable water, we must recognize that all water is holy water. It is also important to painters, since we rely on it as a medium for carrying pigment. For the first ritual, especially, you will need a bowl of water.

Earth. Pigments are gifts from the earth. Though most are now created in laboratories, all colors originally came directly out of the ground. To represent earth on your altar you may want to use a tube of paint, a bowl of earth, a small potted plant, or a vial of soil or sand from a special place.

Air. Feathers are symbols of air. Or the spirit of air can be represented by a song, since our very breath is an expression of that spirit.

Fire. Fire gives us light to work by and passion to work from, and candles are an important part of any altar.

I suggest that whenever you begin a ceremony you take a minute to acknowledge the powers of the elements, and give a brief welcome or thank-you for these gifts that we so often take for granted.

Getting to Work

Cut the box in such a way that it will have a back wall, two side walls, and a floor. This can be done by laying the box on its side, cutting off the top wall, and slitting the two side walls at the bend. You can secure the walls in many ways. You can use tape along the outside walls and under the flooring, and you can glue on extra cardboard pieces as braces.

Cardboard can easily be cut to shape walls or install windows. Use scissors or, best of all, a single-edged blade. X-acto knives are perfect for this job. (Find them in art supply or hardware stores.)

The following is a guide to materials you can use in this project. See resource 1 for details concerning these and other materials.

➢If you want to begin with a white surface, gesso is the best medium for coating the box. Gesso is ground plaster suspended in water. A solidly constructed cardboard box will take layers of gesso very well. Gesso can be diluted with water or used straight from the jar. (It is diluted and applied in layers to minimize the visibility of brush strokes.) Allow each layer of gesso to dry before applying the next coat. As long as you don't saturate the cardboard, it shouldn't warp or weaken. You can paint or glue on cardboard without gesso, but the first few layers of paint will soak into the paper, leaving surface colors dull. Gesso saves using extra coats of paint. It also gives you a clean white surface for drawing, gluing, and so on. Gesso is water fast and will not come off once it is dry.

➢India ink, black paint, or black gesso will give you a black box to work with. India ink applied to the cardboard without a primer (gesso) will be absorbed into the cardboard and may require several coats. Again, allow each coat to dry before applying the next. If you use paint, I suggest an acrylic paint rather than a tempera paint, because acrylics dry to a permanent finish. Water will not permeate or change the acrylic color once it is dry.

➢Collage or glued-on surface treatment can be anything you want. It can be leaves, fabric, postcards, other paintings, old photos, wallpaper, contact paper, sand, shells, mirror pieces, hair (!), or found objects. Consider all possibilities. The three-dimensional format provides a very basic structure for the expression of the personally sacred.

When the Altarpiece Is Finished

You have now created a sacred place. The act of building, of creating a structure, can have a number of repercussions. A three-dimensional piece has a presence that must be acknowledged; it is evidence of your sincerity and a manifestation of your creativity. Unlike a painting, this structure is a place: an altar, a sacred space. Most specifically it is your sacred space. You created it, and it stands as an acknowledgment of your creative potential as well as your new commitment to developing it.

Creating such a space is a primal act. It is an experience you now share with the ancestors who once created such sacred spaces in deserts and mountains. You will probably want to find a specific place in your home for the altarpiece, but keep in mind that just as nomadic people carried sacred objects and altar cloths, you might want to move your altar out into the garden or into another room for special occasions. These structures are light enough to be good travelers.*

You can also create an altar without using the box format. A cloth, a tray, or a pattern drawn in sand can suffice with the inclusion of at least one candle, a bowl of water, and a few personally significant objects.

---

* Altars are wonderful as a place for meditation or as a healing place. In fact, a small bedside altar might be a lovely gift for a sick friend.

Ritual
for a New Beginning

The first pre-requisite for education is a willingness to sacrifice your prejudice on the altar of your spiritual growth.

—LUISAH TEISH *

Once the altarpiece is completed and you have established a site, it's time to consecrate the altar with a ceremony of cleansing and blessing. Judgmental words and attitudes of teachers, relatives, and acquaintances shaped your creative self-image and have lingered for years, embedding old negative messages into the psyche. This ceremony begins with the acknowledgment of those people whom you continue to carry with you, then exorcises their negative ideas, replacing them with the positive voices you may have forgotten.

I recommend painting as a part of this ritual. It adds an immediate experience and affirmation of playfulness and creative potential. At the end of the ritual you may move into the Finger Painting or Breath of God straw-painting project. If you prefer, you can simply play with brilliant water colors or temperas. Whether you choose to paint or do the ritual alone, be sure to allow enough time and private space to get the full benefit of the reflection and ceremony. Keep paper and pencil handy.

Herbs

In the traditions of many indigenous cultures herbs play a traditionally sacred role in ceremonies and rituals. Each herb is believed to have a particular property, which makes it especially appropriate to certain occasions and purposes. An herb still used in the traditional ceremonies of Native American peoples is sage. Sage is endowed with the power of cleansing and transformation. The burning of sage creates a sacred

---

* Luisah Teish, *Jambalaya: The Natural Women's Book of Charms and Practical Rituals* (San Francisco: Harper & Row, 1985), 250.

space as the smoke fills and cleanses the ritual place. The gesture of directing this smoke around the body either with the hand or with a feather prepares the individual to take part in sacred ceremonies. Roman Catholics might find this akin to making the sign of the cross or the burning of incense. Buddhists might liken this practice to the lighting of incense prayer sticks.

For ritual purposes, it's best to burn dried leaf sage, which comes from the plant many of us know as sagebrush. The sage used for cooking is from a different plant; although it will burn, it is more expensive than leaf sage.

Part I:
Beginning the Ceremony—Smudging

The act of burning sage to cleanse a place or person is called *smudging* or *smoking*. It is a Native American custom to begin every ceremony in this way. I suggest that you smudge the area around your altar as a preparation for your opening ceremony. Place the dried sage in a bowl or shell. This should be a receptacle you don't mind getting blackened from the burning; most people keep a special burner just for their smudge. You can keep it on or near the altar.

The sage will not burn for a long time. It will flame and then smolder, giving off a fine, aromatic smoke. If you are alone, you will need only a small amount. You may decide to walk in a circle around your altar, painting work space, or special area. Wave the smoke around the area and then down and around your body, guiding it with your hands. As you breathe gently, imagine a glowing light growing around you. Keeping in mind that you are carrying on an ancient tradition will add to the sacred dimension of this practice. It should never be done frivolously, but with great reverence.

Part II:
Meditation

When you have finished smudging, sit in a comfortable chair and allow yourself to sink into the following guided relaxation and visualization. I suggest that you make a cassette of the meditation text. Use it as frequently as you like. In preparing such a tape, remember to read very slowly and keep a relaxed tone in your voice. Leave pauses in the places where you see the marks ≫ and ≫≫, which suggest spaces for interior processes. ≫ indicates a brief pause, ≫≫ a longer one. If you prefer not to listen to your own voice, ask a friend to do the reading for you. Nevertheless, to acquaint yourself with its format and sequence, read through the full meditation before going into it.

Close your eyes. Breathe deeply and slowly, feeling a warm relaxation pour over your body. From the top of your head, down your neck and shoulders, a glowing, warm comfort enters the muscles and bloodstream. ⟫

With each deep breath, sink deeper and deeper into the dark comfort of your body. ⟫⟫ I must ask you to bring up your negative memories as clearly as possible so that you can more consciously let go of them. I recognize that for some this may be a very difficult and emotional experience, but we must bring those memories into consciousness in order to dissolve their power.

Listen to the voices of the past. ⟫ Hear the phrases that have hurt you. ⟫⟫ See the faces of those who stifled your lively curiosity about the world. ⟫⟫ See yourself as you were then. ⟫⟫ There is no need to hold back tears or anger about these memories. Now is the time to let them out. Do not hold back your weeping; these tears have the power to cleanse your mind of images imposed long ago, images that have imprisoned your creative self in a dungeon of self-doubt. ⟫ Allow the liberation of your creativity through the expression of your true feelings. If you need to carry on an extensive inner dialogue with the person or persons who had the most constricting effect on you, put this cassette on pause now until you are ready to resume. ⟫⟫ *

Having assembled your negative images and their ghostly messages, sit with the smudge bowl in front of you. Relight the sage and, as if the smoke were water, wave it over your body, bathe in it, allow it to cleanse away the negative images that are filling your mind's eye. ⟫ As the sage envelops you, close your eyes and see those images break up and slowly dissipate with the rising smoke. ⟫ The old voices become increasingly faint ⟫ and the images dissolve. ⟫ After the exorcism of these old spirits, you can rest in the dark quietude of your cleansed psyche. ⟫⟫

Now is the time to invite the positive messages you have received over the years to fill this empty space. You may have forgotten these messages, or they may have been overshadowed by demoralizing memories and beliefs. Now, however, there is nothing standing in your way. Spend some time remembering the people who have believed in you and encouraged your work. ⟫ See their faces. ⟫ Hear their voices. ⟫ What exactly did they say to you? ⟫⟫ Feel their strength and support entering you. How do they feel about you reclaiming your creative power? ⟫⟫

In a moment you can pause the tape again, in order to take the time to write yourself a note of affirmation. Your affirmation should be short enough that you will be able to remember it without needing to see it in writing. With this brief

---

* When the meditation is over, you may want to write that person (or those persons) a letter. You don't need to mail it; just writing it will be helpful.

affirmation acknowledge your courage and your ability to reclaim and enjoy your creativity. Here are a few examples:

- *I am expanding my creative potential every day.*
- *I am increasingly courageous and original in my creative expression.*
- *I have all the permission I need to be a fully creative and unique person.*
- *I am as creative as any other person; I just need to let my natural abilities flow.*

Pause the tape now, until you're ready to resume.

Set your written affirmation on the altar. You may want to copy it later onto three-by-five cards and put it in places where you will find it unexpectedly from time to time. Affirmations are most effective when they turn up suddenly.

Now repeat the affirmation out loud. Say it again, aware of how good it feels to hear your own positive voice.

You will remember this meditation each time you begin to paint, and each time you read or speak this affirmation. You are reclaiming your creativity, playfulness, and spiritual delight. Congratulations!

[End tape here.]

Part III:
A Yoruba Blessing

The next part of this ceremony is a blessing from the African Yoruba tradition. It is adapted from Luisah Teish's book *Jambalaya*.* It is a blessing of the head, where three important forces are centered. The three areas are as follows:

1. The top of the head, the *ache* (pronounced *aw-chay*), is the seat of personal power given to each person at birth.
2. The back of the head at the base of the brain, known in Yoruba as the *eshu ni baco*, is considered to be a doorway to the spirit of Elegba, a mischievous deity who causes us to be confused, misguided, or unreasonably suspicious. I consider this a seat of self-doubt.
3. The area between the eyebrows, *eleda*, the "little creator," is a source of inspiration and clarity.

---

* Teish, *Jambalaya*, 216.

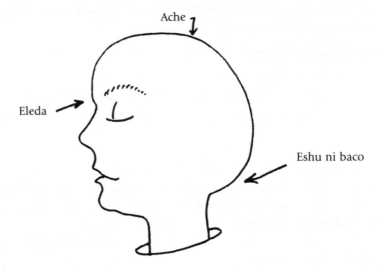

Ache

Eleda

Eshu ni baco

According to Teish, it is important to maintain a balanced interaction between the three forces. The *ache* generates energy and can be replenished and refreshed through ritual. The other two respond well to frequent cleansing, so you may want to reenact this ritual from time to time.

The ritual is called a *rogacion,* a traditional cleansing in orthodox Afro-diasporic practice. I have adapted it for the Creative Meditation process to focus on creativity. Administering this *rogacion,* these symbolic prayerful gestures of blessing the three head centers with water, is your first act of personal creative empowerment.

Administering the Rogacion

Place the tip of the index finger into the water on your altar. Placing that fingertip on the top of your head, the place of *ache,* take a moment to recognize the gift of energy that keeps you moving and productive. Recognize this spot at the top of your head as the place where you were touched by the divine when you were blessed with life. In your gratitude and celebration of this energy, envision a white light glowing there. See your energy flowing and pure.

Place your fingertip once again in the water, this time touching lightly the back of your neck. This is the place where self-doubts and negative thoughts can enter your psyche, so imagine fortifying this place. The sage has cleansed away previous malevolent energies, so you are now able to reaffirm yourself. Say your affirmation three times aloud. Be sure that you hear and receive this affirmation. Picture it implanted at the base of your neck, the *eshu ni baco.* Let this affirmation be your shield against the entry of negative voices, old or new. If you hear negative phrases or ideas, imagine that shield deflecting all words not empowering to you.

For the last blessing, place your fingertips in the water again and touch the space between your eyebrows. The *eleda,* which is referred to as "the third eye" in some Eastern meditation practices, is the place of vision. Give a brief thank-you for the images and creations that you have already given birth to in your life. You have already envisioned and created many things—Your home, your children, the type of work you do, the meals you bring to your table, clothing, gardens, etc. Spend some time seeing those creations in your mind's eye, recognizing that each one is evidence of your creative powers.

Inherent Affirmation

In closing, focus on your hands. Turn them in all directions. Bend and straighten the fingers, touch fingertips together, and finally pick up your pencil.

These hands are the result of millions of years of evolution. The ability to pick up a pencil, as you just did, is the gift of every human who ever fought to stay alive. As creativity and tenacity continue to save our species from extinction, your willingness to create confirms that the centuries of struggle that have brought us this far have not been in vain. Every creation, from the simplest watercolor to the finest masterpiece, is a timeless statement of humanity saying "Yes I can!"

With this in mind, end your ceremony with a brief but empowering closing phrase, such as "May my images be plentiful and provocative." This phrase, or a similar one, may become a personal tradition for your Creative Meditation closure.

When this ritual is done in groups, it is ended with name singing. To do this alone, simply sing your name in any musical configuration or pattern that spontaneously comes to you. It is a beautiful experience to hear and express your name as a song.

Releasing the Power of Childhood

And even if you found yourself in some prison, whose walls let in none of the world's sounds—wouldn't you still have your childhood, that jewel beyond all price, that treasure house of memories? Turn your attention to it. Try to raise up the sunken feelings of this enormous past; your personality will grow stronger, your solitude will expand and become a place where you can live in the twilight, where the noise of other people passes by, far in the distance. And if out of this turning-within, out of this immersion in your own world, poems come, then you will not think of asking anyone whether they are good or not.

RAINER MARIA RILKE

With the making of the altarpiece and the completion of the first ceremony, we have taken the first steps toward freeing your creative spirit. We have invoked the radiance of divinity within you and reconnected with the inherent affirmation of the ancestors. Our next step is to release the power of childhood stored within you. Read the following sentence and think about it for a moment with your eyes closed.

Listening to the sound of children giggling stirs my own joyous childhood memories.

When I recall the sound of children giggling I want to smile. Did that happen to you? With eyes closed, go back into that space for a minute longer, and recall some playful moments of your own childhood. Remember being tickled? or chased by a friend? rolling around on the grass? Below is a space to record one of your favorite memories. By writing it down you can use it as a doorway into your childhood memory bank; use it as a touchstone with the past.

Record your memory here:

The Dance of Energies

The creative process is a dance of energies, a process of guided chance. At times the dance is a waltz, gliding along with natural grace in a gradual unfolding of movements. At other times, the dance is a polka, whirling us through time and space until we come to rest in breathless exhilaration. Sometimes, however, the dance feels awkward, the music seems hard to hear, the dance floor is too crowded. At these times, we must maintain self-respect, compassion, and trust in the natural rhythms of the universe. When we begin with an acknowledgment of the creative process as a divine mystery, which is the same for neophyte and virtuoso alike, we realize that the capacity for creativity is a common denominator among people. It is our willingness, our daring, to explore it and to dedicate ourselves to it that determines our fate as individuals and as a species. Whether the creative dance is fast or slow, it is always exhilarating.

Exercise:
Finger Painting

To celebrate the creative play of childhood, enjoy something you may not have experienced for many years: finger painting! This is a creative activity you can enjoy over and over again. While some people are delighted by this prospect, some scoff, and others are only mildly amused. In the end the experience almost always turns out to be amazingly rewarding and definitely fun. Those who have never finger painted find it a very freeing experience. Others find that it brings back important childhood memories buried under the struggles of adulthood. For some, the rewards come in surprising insights days or weeks after the experience.

Recognizing that for some childhood was a difficult time, I have designed a process for sharing uncomfortable memories with a partner, or recording them into a tape recorder. I suggest you consider finger painting with a good friend or a therapist if you are afraid of dredging up something unpleasant. In fact, you might consider doing it twice: once on your own, and then with one or more friends.

Caveat: do not finger paint for the first time with children. You need to invite your own inner child to play. When children are present, you are an adult. You should feel free of responsibility to others while you are finger painting. Give yourself a free zone in which to work and play.* If you have children who want to play too, set up another time to paint with them.

When you work alone, I suggest that you use some playful music to get you in the mood. Whether painting alone or with a partner, use a tape recorder so you can capture free associations as they come. (It's possible each person will want his or her own cassette for reflection, so you may want to use two recorders.) Please read all the instructions and guidelines before beginning.

---

* If you have trouble protecting your creative space, turn to chapter 5 and follow the meditation for establishing a doorkeeper. A doorkeeper is a dimension of your own psyche that can stand watch and guard your privacy during work periods.

Supplies

* Finger paint
* Polymer medium (optional)
* Oil cloth
* Paper towel
* Paper
* Bowls or bucket of water
* Masking tape
* Scissors
* Tape recorder and cassette for recording
* Music player and long-playing music cassette (do not use a radio station) (Optional)

Finger paints can usually be found in any art supply store, or in toy stores, often in kits. They are very inexpensive. Special finger paint paper can also be purchased, or you can buy rolls of shiny white shelf paper—it's very cheap and works very well.

Finger paint will flake off the paper when it dries, but you can prevent this by mixing a bit of polymer medium (see resource 1) with each color. It dries transparent and will act as a binder to stop the flaking. (Even though I don't want to encourage a product-oriented approach to this work, when you have finished with your Creative Meditation experiences of finger painting, you may find yourself with some highly original wrapping paper!)

If you decide to mix your finger paints with polymer medium, do this before you begin painting. Transfer the paint from its original container to a jar with a tight-fitting lid. Add polymer medium at the ratio of one part medium to four parts paint. This medium will make the color more transparent, so don't add too much—just use enough to bind the paint. If four to one seems to make the color too thin, use less polymer. Mix thoroughly. Keep any unused medium and paint tightly capped and out of the reach of children or pets. Containers and tools can be washed with soap and water, as the finger paints and polymer are water soluble.

Finger painting is best done on a table. Be sure to put some type of covering on your work table so that you will not be inhibited about making large gestures or going off the page. A large piece of oil cloth is ideal, as it can be easily washed.

Have plenty of paper handy and ready to go. If you have decided to work with a roll of shiny shelf paper, have sections precut. Keep a roll of masking tape handy. Tape down the corners of each piece before you begin working.

How to Proceed

➤Place open paints in front of you so that all colors are easily accessible. Have the large bowl of water handy, as well as cloth or paper towels.

➤Don't forget to have your tape recorder ready to record any free associations or other thoughts. I suggest that you place a tab of masking tape over each button, so that you can pause and record at will without having to clean your fingers each time.

A Special Word About Breathing

Try to remain conscious of your breathing. Get into the habit of beginning your painting and drawing experiences with several slow, deep breaths. Closing your eyes during these breaths helps to calm the mind and body, facilitating your focus and serenity. With each breath, place your focus at the base of your nose and flare your nostrils. This will make you more aware of opening yourself up to new images. I think of this as developing a hospitable mind. Deep breathing actually enhances our capacity for creativity by increasing the flow of blood and oxygen within the body.

Air is our primary and most immediate source of empowerment. As you breathe, allow your belly to expand down into your groin. Each time you begin to work, be sure to breathe consciously and deeply. Breathing is as important to creative activity as it is to strenuous physical activity. Most of the time we breathe shallowly, so it will be important for you to think about your breathing from time to time.

You will find that this breathing technique is helpful wherever you go. It is an excellent way to get centered and calm. (I will remind you to breathe creatively from time to time in the instructions, just in case you forget.)

Working with a Partner

In working with a partner, you must first decide who this person will be. It must be someone you trust. While it may be very interesting to do this with a sibling or childhood friend, there may be certain things you would be uncomfortable revealing to or discussing with them at first. Choose someone you feel totally accepted by, someone with whom you can play and cry. Certainly this must be someone who is also willing to take part joyfully and who trusts you enough to be self-revealing.

Set up your work space across from each other. Place the tape recorder(s) between you. You may work standing or sitting, but I highly recommend standing, because it allows greater and freer expression to the entire body. Sitting is one more thing you learned in school.

Getting to Work

Use the following questions and suggestions to facilitate your process. Put on some music if you like, adjusting the volume so as not to interfere with recording your voice. When you are ready to begin, check in with your body. Do some conscious breathing, and turn on the tape recorder.

➤Talk to your partner about how your body feels. How did you relate to your body when you were a child?

➤As the body dialogue develops between you, begin to paint.

➤Allow your feelings and memories to determine the colors you use and the lines created by your hands. Remember the things you did with your hands in childhood. Did you play marbles or jacks? Did you make mud pies? Your hands have memories stored in the muscles; allow them to remember their childhood.

Individual Work

When you are finger painting alone, try to keep talking without controlling or censoring your thoughts. If you are having trouble bringing back childhood memories, start by talking about your lack of memory. Go to an event, a singular memory or person that was important to you. Keep talking. Allow single words to come out, or names. These will connect to something. Follow the words and images. Moving your body while you are talking activates both hemispheres of your brain. This type of simultaneous activity may help you to regain some memories that would not have been available in a static form of meditation. Follow this format until you feel finished with your first painting. If you feel that you want to pursue this material further, set up another sheet of paper and continue.

I suggest you take a break from time to time. Give your body a chance to stretch and your mind a chance to relax and wander. Get some fresh air, go for a walk. Remember that bending over a table for half an hour or so will put stress on your back. Do some gentle stretching, and change postures from time to time.

To proceed, I suggest that you use the same format as above, selecting a topic or just talking and asking questions of yourself and/or of your partner. Our childhood is such a rich treasury of memories that almost any topic will be a gateway to self-revelation and creativity.

Keep in mind that this exercise is not merely a method of making pictures. The important thing is to have a real body experience. I encourage you to explore the use of your hands as tools. They can imprint forms; they can create patterns, lines, scratches. Finger painting has a tremendous freedom and potential for the abstract expression of emotions. Take advantage of this. Play!

Some Subjects for Thought or Discussion

➤My favorite activity as a kid was:

➤What I hated most about my childhood:

➤When I was a kid I loved to eat:

➤My attitudes toward my parents, and how they changed with different ages and events:

➤School: academics and teachers, sports, social scene, romances:

➤Family: favorite relatives, best or worst memories, holidays:

➤Parts of my childhood that I carried into adulthood:

Keep in mind that the creative process is a dynamic combination of making something happen and letting something happen. That is also the dynamic of dance: leading and following. In painting, the medium is your partner, and you will need to learn ways of following it. Be patient and relax. Just as you can't push your dance partner around, paint needs space to move in its own natural manner. Let it teach you about how it likes to move and flow.

Many people are under the impression that professional artists have complete control of medium and images. Nothing could be further from the truth. The variables are too numerous to count. While I might be well acquainted with the basic nature of my medium, I am never quite sure how certain compositional elements or colors might react to each other. I often try doing something new with the medium, and I can't predict how it will react. Art is not science—it's art! Creativity is an organic, spontaneous process. You may feel more comfortable with the uncertainty of the process by reading the candid admissions of the English painter Francis Bacon, considered by many to have been one of the greatest painters of the twentieth century.

> I know what I want to do, but I don't know how to do it. And I look at them almost like a stranger, not knowing how these things have come about and why have these marks that have happened on the canvas evolved into these particular forms. And then, of course, I remember what I wanted to do and I do, of course, try then and push these irrational forms into what I originally wanted to do.*

Once you have created some of your own paintings, you'll have a better understanding of the creative risk taking and spiritual explorations that go into each piece. You'll understand that because paintings are exhibited only when they're finished, it's easy to imagine that they were easily conceived and executed. Embarking on your own creative exploration will help you appreciate the creations of others in an entirely new way.

Play: *The Dance of Possibilities*

If the creative process is a dance of energies, then play is a dance of possibilities. Take a few moments to go back to your early memories of play. Do

---

* David Sylvester, *The Brutality of Fact: Interview with Francis Bacon* (New York: Thames & Hudson, 1987), 100.

There is nothing more seriously connected with our deepest longing than is our play.

M. C. RICHARDS

you remember playing at the beach or in a sandbox? Remember making mud pies, and turning cartwheels? If you think back to the time when you played without a game board or scoring system, you will probably remember being silly and curious. Like the characters in C. S. Lewis's classic, *The Lion, the Witch, and the Wardrobe*, young children when left to their own devices will wander and explore their environment for play themes and activities. Even though most children are not taken as far as Narnia, the imagination is no doubt the earliest vehicle for the transportation of the human spirit.

Real play, the mud pie version, is goalless. It is the mind meandering from one thing to the next, in a constant process of acceptance and movement. Without the game format, play has no winner or loser. Play is the dance of possibilities performed by the agile human mind. It encompasses textural experience, intellectual curiosity, creative activity, and the exhilaration of discovery. You could say that play is the central ingredient in the transformational abilities of our species. Spiritually, it is the sacred celebration of our spontaneous engagement with the world around us.

A good example of adult play in an artistic medium is improvisational theater. Improvisation has no learned lines, no script, nor predetermined direction. It rests upon spontaneous interaction. It requires courage, excellent communication skills, and spontaneous imaginative response. I once heard "improv" described as a "yes, and . . ." process. This "yes, and . . ." mind-set is the opposite of "yes, but. . . ." The former is a key to creativity, because it accepts everything and adds to it. A "yes, but . . ." mind-set suggests the acceptance of a given situation, followed by a barrier. The "but" is a stop sign. It brings the creative process to a halt. When you say "yes, but" you are disengaging your energy, refusing to take part, refusing to allow a new thing to grow.

Exercise:
The Breath of God

In the following painting experience you will see firsthand how this improvisational play process takes place on paper with colorful inks. Whether working alone or with others, remember to read through all the directions before beginning.

I learned the basic format of this exercise from Blanche Gallagher, my talented friend and colleague from Chicago. I named it "The Breath of God" because it is a beautiful experience of how creative our breath can be even without speaking or singing. The meditation above has already helped you to realize how breath is the essence and empowerment of our life and work. This project proves that even if you can't carry a tune, your breath can paint a song.

Supplies

* Brilliant water colors (see resource 1). You should have a minimum of three colors: red, blue, and yellow. You will find these available in many shades, so try to select shades that you would like to see together on a page. Black makes a dramatic addition, so you may want to use India ink as well. It is actually best to stay away from using too many colors at the beginning, because they may become muddy on the page. You can always add new colors later. (I'm very aware of the expense of art supplies, and you will be, too, after your first trip to an art supply store.)
* An eye dropper. Some inks come with eye droppers; if those you are using don't have them, use a separate one for each ink, with its own supply of fresh water for cleaning it out. Don't let colors contaminate each other. They will mix together on the page.

* Paper. Watercolor paper works best, but if your budget does not allow it, an all-purpose white drawing paper will work well. Minimum size: fifteen by twenty inches. Do not use newsprint, cardboard, or anything too absorbent.
* Straws. I prefer bendable straws, but any regular drinking straw will do.
* Plastic containers of assorted sizes. Develop a collection of plastic (yogurt and cottage cheese, etc.) containers. They are nonrecyclable, and using them over and over for painting projects is at least one way to expand their usefulness on the planet.
* Paper towels and rags. Ecologically, washable rags or towels are best.
* Cotton balls and liquid bleach (optional). Bleach is the only medium that has the power to remove these colors (even when dry), so if one can stand the toxic presence of bleach, it can add an extra dimension to the possibilities of the form. You will use it sparingly. I recommend using an odorless bleach. Keep it in small glass containers, as it can eat through some paper containers. Keep it capped when not in use, and *do not use it if you're painting with children.* Also keep in mind that while brushes are not desirable for this exercise, if you ever use bleach with a brush you should know that bleach will eat away the bristles. You might try diluting it and keeping the brush in water when not in use. I suggest experimenting with the cheapest brush you can find.

     Note: Once you begin blow painting, bleach should be introduced only after a composition has begun to form.

Preparation

Prepare:
* One sheet of paper
* Brilliant watercolors (one of each color available)
* One or two empty containers or saucers for mixing and diluting
* One or two containers of water
* A straw
* Paper towels
* Music and music player

How to Proceed

Once you are set up, put on a fairly lengthy piece of music that you find especially beautiful; a single side of a record or cassette should be sufficient. The music should be something classical, meditative, or inspiring. Stay away from things that have sentimental value, as such music can invoke old images, memories, and feelings that will rob you of the spontaneous interaction of music and paint translated through the human body. Remember that not only your head and hands make art: the muscle and bone of your entire body go into painting.

With the music playing, stand comfortably or get comfortable in your seat. Close your eyes and take a slow, deep breath. Give your body a moment to be still. Focus on a dark, calm spot deep in the center of your body. As you breathe, allow the tension in your neck and shoulders to melt away. As you relax, surrender to the music, feeling it pulsing through your body. Slowly open your eyes and take in the whiteness of the page before you. Let the music guide you in your choice of a color to begin.

Caveat: It is possible to hyperventilate by blowing too long or too hard. Hyperventilation can cause dizziness, lightheadedness, or a seemingly altered state of consciousness. Don't blow too hard into the straw, and be aware of any pigments that may make their way back up the straw. *Never breathe in through the straw; always blow out.* Take a rest every now and then to keep your head clear.

Getting to Work

With the eye dropper place a small amount of the color on the paper and blow it around on the page with the straw. Keep the straw about one-quarter to one-half inch off the page, and direct the trajectory of the color by moving the straw and/or the paper as you work.

Continue adding the various colors in response to the mood and rhythm of the music. Frequent rest periods not only help to keep you from getting fuzzy-headed but also allow you to evaluate what's happening on the page.

You can also add a drop of water from time to time, blowing it, or tilting the paper to let it run and blend colors in different directions. Brilliant watercolors are optically very exciting, and they're fun to play with. Enjoy spending time with them. These bright pigments are very transparent, and compositions can become an intriguing matrix of layered color and line. Sometimes recognizable forms will develop; at other times the image will be abstract. Don't try to control the image into a recognizable form—just let it happen.

Don't use a brush. Blowing the watercolors with a straw gives a great sense of freedom, and the lack of control relieves you of any preexisting expectations you may have of yourself. This is a free-form exercise, a time to be playful; it has no goal other than the pleasure of doing it.

At some point you may want to stop to let the page dry. Take a break from the optical excitement. Go for a walk.

When you return, look at the page in silence. Can you hear the music by looking at the page? Ask yourself what you would like to do next. If you are working with bleach, you might want to introduce it at this point. It can be applied either with a cotton ball or swab, or in thin lines with the end of the straw. You can drip some onto the page and blow it around as you did the pigments. (Do I need to remind you not to inhale? . . . Don't inhale!)

Work until you feel finished, with or without music.

Every time I engage in the Breath of God exercise, I feel enchanted. I feel as if the child within me were awakened by the optical excitement of those colors exploding and slithering all over that white page. It reminds me of the fireworks on the Fourth of July. It's an excellent way to have fun and loosen up. Keep it in mind as a warm-up or as play practice. Like all of the exercises and projects in this book, it can be done over and over again.

The sense of delight this exercise gives is one of the aspects of Creative Meditation that I love, because it connects me with the feelings of my childhood, rather than intellectual ideas or memories. Creativity is the sacred gift that allows us access to a constantly available source of enlightenment, challenge, and joy.

Exercise:
Reflection #2

Many of our personal beliefs about creativity and self-image have developed uncon-sciously over the span of a lifetime. Without questioning or evaluating these beliefs or their origins, we continue to be ruled by them.

Take time to reflect on the following questions. Understanding is an important step in freeing the creative spirit. You may realize that you have been living in a false personal mythology that does not promote your creativity.

➤What assumptions do I have about "creative people"?

➤Where did I get those ideas? Do I really believe them or are they things I have come to accept?

➤Do I think of myself as creative? Do I believe I am creative only in certain situations?

➤What stops me from seeing myself as creative in all situations?

➤Do I believe that there is a creative seed inside me that could become a dynamic part of my life?

➤What is standing in the way of developing my creativity?

➤How can I overcome my obstacles?

Our daily lives are a constant creative undertaking. Product and process are indivisible, a dynamic cycle of solution and celebration. Take some time to think about the ways you are creative in your daily life. You make creative decisions daily. Consider these:

- Wardrobe
- Meal planning and nutrition
- Work-related problem solving
- Relationships
- Finances and budgeting
- Entertainment

In the space below, make a list of the ways you already exercise your creativity.

Like the styles of movie directors and producers, each person's work grows from a fundamentally unique perspective. The films of Steven Spielberg, for example, are very different from those of Francis Ford Coppola. Every person has a distinct quality to her or his work. It will be helpful to remember that as you see your own style emerging after you've been drawing and painting for a while.

Sit down in a quiet place and think back to memories of elementary school. Do you remember how you learned to judge yourself? After you have gone through your memories once, go back to them. This time imagine that you, as an affirming adult, are standing beside yourself as a child. Tell this child the things you wish someone had said to you.

That child still lives within you. Say these things to your adult self. Say them aloud. Write them down.

If you know elementary-school-age children, watch them work, or engage them in conversation. Can you see if they are being taught this pattern of self-criticism? Give them the message you wish someone had given you.

Exercise:
Drawing Page

Reflecting on your childhood, think of the pictures you created. Get out your crayons, and in the space provided, draw a picture of your home and family as you might have drawn it at the age of six. You can play with this idea in your journal, but don't be intimidated about putting it into this book as well.

Exercise:
Getting Acquainted with Paint

This exercise is designed to give you a little practice with tempera paint. Taking some time to play and become acquainted with the medium will help you to relax and have fun as you go along with the exercises ahead.

Supplies

* Paper—large
* Tempera paint—use any three colors you wish, plus black and white. Put about a tablespoon of each onto a palette.
* Water in containers (two sixteen-ounce containers, or something equivalent)
* Two brushes: one pointed, large #6 and one flat-edge two- or three-inch wash brush
* A sponge
* Paper towels or absorbent rags
* Oil cloth for surface protection

How to Proceed

➤Lay out the paper on a large work table or on the floor. You will be using a lot of water, so if you need to protect the work surface use the oil cloth.

➤Once you are set up, take a minute to close your eyes and follow your breath deep into your body. Get in touch with your tensions and feelings.

➤When you feel ready—take as much time as you need—take the wash brush deliberately in your dominant hand. Dip it into the water and brush it broadly across the paper. Do this several times, feeling the movement of your body.

➤Select one of your colors according to its ability to best express your mood. Make some continuous brush strokes of this color broadly across the paper, feeling the movement of your shoulder blades. If you are standing, sit down and make the next strokes in another color, feeling the difference in your posture and muscle movement. If you were sitting, stand, and do the same.

➤Clean off the brush and make a few more strokes with water. Keeping the page very wet will not allow a great deal of control, and this, of course, is the idea. Focus on the process, the dance of painting, rather than the image developing on the page.

➤While you're working, focus on all the things you love about yourself. No one else needs to know what you're thinking. This can be anything from the shape of your fingers, or your generosity, to the dream you had last night. Let no other thoughts into your mind. Focus on the things you love about yourself.

➤When you've worked with the flat-edge brush for a while, set it in the water and use the pointed brush. Your hand will know immediately that you are doing something new. Feel the difference in your hand muscles.

➤Try some splattering motions. Try holding the brush close to the fibers and then at the end of the handle. Remember to keep returning to the water to keep the page wet and the paint in motion.

➤Continue to paint for as long as you like, mingling colors and exploring different body movements. If the page becomes impossibly wet and weakened, allow it to dry for a while. Take a break and come back in fifteen to thirty minutes. You might want to spend some time writing about the experience. We're very seldom asked to dwell on our positive aspects. How did it feel? Was it hard to do?

➤Resume or discontinue your work as you wish. These paintings are your classroom. Experiment daubing a dry or wet sponge across the surface. See what kind of textures or lines you can get from the sponge edges. Experiment with the amount of paint on the brush, or build up the amount by layering it on the page.

➤In your painting journal, take some time to record your experience and discoveries. Here are some questions to guide your reflection process:

- What did you learn about your body? Your emotions?

- About water and paint?

- What did you learn about the two brushes? About the sponge?

- What did you learn about the paper?

- Anything else?

This painting process is just a beginning. If you are not happy with the results, remember that the real results are not on the page. The painting was a success because it gave you an experience you had never had. You can see that with only a few simple tools you can go deeply into a part of yourself that you might not otherwise have touched. I hope you've had some fun as well.

Each time you come to this process, which I hope you will do often, consciously push on the margins of your possibilities. Use different tools, or use them in a new way. Use your body in a different way. Don't be afraid to get your hands dirty, or your elbows. Use kitchen utensils or any other implements that you think might have an interesting effect.

This expansion of the creative process will feed into other avenues of self-expansion as you become more self-confident. That confidence will lead to a greater self-expressive autonomy and technical ability.

CHAPTER TWO

Reflections
in the Inner Well

FROM WITHIN THE depths of every individual a wisdom is flowing. Its source is darkness: the mysteries of psyche and soul. These are the mysteries of personal origin as well as future possibilities, and only the courage to look into the well of self-knowledge, the willingness to contemplate our own darkness, can reveal such mysteries to us.

Unfortunately, we live in a dualistic society that has taught us not only fear of the dark, but disbelief about the fundamental goodness of our deepest nature. The idea of delving into our inner well, therefore, can be a frightening and challenging proposition for some. At the core of this challenge I see a question of love. In essence, Creative Meditation is based upon the belief that the universe has been loved into existence, and that creativity is our ongoing participation in that love.

This means that all creation is based upon affirmation, based upon *yes*. All we see are the things that life has said "yes" to, and yes is an expression of acceptance. This does not mean that there is no violence in the world, nor that ugliness and injustice do not exist. They exist because the universe accepts them as the balance points to peace and harmony. Even the things we hate and fight against remain as the catalysts of courageous accomplishment.

Chapter 1 established a new foundation for creative activity by first reconnecting us with our spiritual and evolutionary roots, and then reclaiming the childhood memories of our personal self. If we are to accept ourselves as sacred beings, we must be able to go further into ourselves, into the resonance of divinity within our lives. When we see that divinity is an affectionate breath of generative energy, we open our eyes to the love within and around ourselves.

While this may seem a romantic view of life and divinity, the evidence surrounds us. Feel the breeze caress your skin. Listen to the music of leaves rustling. Look at the morning dew adorning a spider's web. Every child is born from the darkness of the womb, every leaf from the dark stem of the plant. In this chapter we will explore the creative resources that are constantly flowing out from our own darkness.

In art, as in life, everything is possible so long as it is based on love.

MARC CHAGALL

Exercise:
Love Paintings

I'm always perplexed by people asking me how I come up with ideas for my paintings. This, to me, is like asking parents how they came up with their children. Paintings grow from the process of loving. The moment you put something, anything, on a surface it's like an embryo moving toward greater life. My paintings, like the rest of the universe, are loved into existence.

To dive into the experience of divinity we have discussed, this exercise will focus on sinking deep into yourself as a manifestation of the divine love that creates the universe. Keep in mind that just as a loving relationship with a person sometimes requires work and struggle, your relationship with painting and drawing will remain an emotionally challenging activity.

In the love paintings, I'd like you to focus on loving your images into being. Embrace the sense memories locked into your body; use as little thought as possible. The divinity at your core is the central love that created you and from which you continue creating.

Supplies

For Painting I

* Blue and red finger paint and paper, water, towels, etc. (same setup as for previous finger-paint exercises)
* Music: a favorite piece

For Painting II

* Tempera paint, crayons, brushes, watercolor pencils, watercolor crayons, anything you enjoy working with
* Large paper: vellum, watercolor, or butcher paper
* The usual paraphernalia: water, containers, rags or paper towels, etc.
* Music: a favorite piece or something that is related somehow to the person you select for your meditation

Getting to Work

Painting I

➤Carve some space into your weekly routine for a miniretreat. (This is unquestionably the most difficult part of this exercise!) During this time, which should be no less than four hours (a whole day would be great), you will not answer the phone, listen to family members, worry about bills, or do anything outside of the meditation. While I hope this has been true for all your painting experiences, this project is designed to be a time of deep reflection and healing.

➤You may want to begin with a walk or a trip to the seaside. Whichever route to tranquillity you choose, when you get there take a few minutes to get in touch with your body, your breathing, and your natural rhythm. Sink into your relationship with God. Think about Eros, the loving, even sensuous, side of God. How do you experience this dimension of the divine in your life? For many people this is an area of great alienation.

➤While sitting alone in this quiet contemplation, open the palms of your hands as they sit in your lap. Bring the palms toward your face and really look at them. Touch your skin. Feel the folds, the calluses, and lines. Touch your nails. These hands are manifestations of the erotic God. When we are whole, and our body is well, we tend to take it for granted. When it suffers through illness or loss, we suddenly realize its beauty and godliness. If you were to lose the sensation in just one finger you would experience a deep deprivation and sorrow. If you have already lost some function of your hands, take this time to appreciate your recovery and continuing capacity to meet physical challenges. Enjoy this time to celebrate the beauty and wonder of your body. Your hands are creators, lovers, healers. They are a manifestation of Eros. Think about all the people they touch and have touched. Relive the sense memories locked into the muscles of your hands.

➤When you have spent a good deal of time reminiscing, lay out your paper and paints. With your favorite music playing, slowly put your fingers into the paint. In order to really feel the body of the paint, close your eyes. Rub the paint between your hands. Then slowly begin to caress the paper with your fingers and knuckles. Use as many different parts of your hands as possible as you sink deeply into this sensuous experience of muscle, bone, and paint.

➤Continue this process until you feel finished. It doesn't matter at all what this piece looks like, as long as you had an enjoyable time doing it.

Painting II

➤During this painting, focus your attention on one important person in your life. After you have done the usual relaxed breathing and centering, go back to the very earliest memories you have of this person. Spend some time going deeply into the feelings you've had through the evolution of your relationship. What is the general color scheme of your relationship? If it has always been a very emotional or passionate relationship, it might be reds and oranges, very hot colors. If it has been a respectful relationship with a strong intellectual component, the colors might be on the cool side, grays and blues. If it has varied with time, what color is it now?

➤Using those colors as a starting point, begin a painting that expresses some of your feelings toward this person and the love you experience coming from him or her. Do not make this a narrative painting about your relationship. You may choose to do that at a later date, but for now stay with your feelings and body sensations. Experiment with jagged line and curved line, large strokes and small strokes. Use as many different media as you like. You may want to begin with crayons or watercolor pencil; you can do whatever feels natural. If you feel that you have lost the feeling, stop working for a moment and go back into your body with rhythmic breathing and closed eyes. Return to the memory of your loved one as a continuing inspiration.

➤As you progress through this book the world will expand. In reality, of course, the expansion will be in yourself. Learning to see yourself with new eyes will also bring a new vision of the world around you. You will become more intimate with the world, increasing your ability to receive all that longs to reveal itself. You will caress the world with loving eyes.

Ceremony
of Self-Affirmation

Self-affirming rituals are sadly missing from the regularly scheduled lives of most people. Do the following ceremony in its complete form first, and perform it as frequently as you like. You can also design a shorter daily ritual from it.

Supplies

* White candle, sage or other incense if desired, journal, comfortable pillow(s)
* Photographs: Bring to your altar some photographs of yourself, especially from your childhood. Choose a picture you feel good about, or that has special memories. Any number will do. If you are having strange feelings about doing this, realize that those feelings are manifestations of the deep limitations squelching your capacity for self-acceptance and creativity. Pushing past these limitations is a challenge.

   The photo-gathering process may take some time. You might also collect photos of people you admire, or those who believe in you. These may be personal acquaintances or well-known figures. I refer to such people as my saints, their presence encourages me when self-doubts come up.

Getting to Work

➤When you have collected your photos, place them on the altar and light a white candle. Burn sage for cleansing. If you have established another incense for ceremonial times, light that at this time. Sit comfortably before the altar.

➤Silently say your name. Repeat it. Repeat it again. Voice it. Say your name aloud again and again until it becomes a constant pattern without stopping, like a mantra (an Eastern meditation prayer). Continue the mantra for two minutes.

➤At the end of the two minutes let silence take its place for another full minute.

➤Now read the following poem, by the thirteenth century poet, Rumi, silently or aloud:

> You should try to hear the name the Holy One has for things.
> There is something in the phrase: "The Holy One has taught him names."
> We name everything according to the number of legs it has;
> the other one names it according to what it has inside.
> Moses waved his stick; he thought it was a "rod,"
> but inside its name was "dragonish snake."
> We thought the name of Blake was "agitator against priests,"
> but in eternity his name is "the one who believes."
> No one knows our name until our last breath goes out.*

➤With a journal and pen or pencil at hand, meditate on your name.

- What connections do you have to your name?
- How do you feel about it?
- Are you like Moses' stick? Do people call you by the wrong name?
- Is there a name you feel is really you? What is that name?

➤When you know your name, sing it aloud. Sing it over and over in any melodic line you choose. Look at the pictures on the altar and sing your name into those images.

➤Finally, whisper it. Whisper your name with your eyes closed, feeling it in your head. Send your name deep into your body. Sit for a minute in silence, absorbing the wonderful feeling of knowing your name and being this person.

---

* Version by Robert Bly, *News of the Universe: Poems of a Twofold Consciousness* (San Francisco: Sierra Club Books, 1980), 268.

Exercise:
The Signature Beyond a Name

Now that you know your name, let's return to doing some creative work with your signature. If you'd like to continue with your regular signature, feel free to do so. Just as we are stretching your image of yourself, the following exercise will allow you to stretch your name into abstract paintings.

Supplies

* Sturdy vellum drawing/multipurpose paper. I use a paper called Mohawk Super-fine. It comes in individual sheets, forty by twenty-six inches. If you cannot find sturdy paper in this large size, use smaller paper taped together according to the directions below.
* Masking tape—one-half- to three-fourths-inch width
* Watercolor crayons, one regular wax crayon, and tempera paints in primary colors (red, yellow, and blue) plus white and black
* Assorted brushes
* Polymer gloss medium (optional)
* Palette, water containers, paper towels, or rags

Getting to Work

➤If you're working with small sheets of paper, mask together three sheets of drawing paper along the long sides (edge to edge), so they create one sheet the length of three widths. There should be no masking tape visible on the side you will be working on.

➤Repeat this with three more sheets.

➤Mask the two large sheets together lengthwise on the already taped side.

➤You will now have one large surface consisting of six panels. There should be no spaces between any of the panels and no visible masking tape when the large page is turned with the working surface facing you. If you have one large sheet, you will eventually cut that sheet into these six panels.

➤Set up your work space. Be sure that your paper is on an unobstructed, consistent surface, and be sure that you have ample room for large gestures.

➤Stand in front of your work table, or if you're kneeling on the floor, make sure to pad your knees and make your legs comfortable. A prayer or meditation stool can be very helpful for floor work. It is about the height of a low footstool but has a slanted seat that your legs can fit under when kneeling. If you cannot stand or kneel, be sure that your table space allows as much freedom of movement as you need.

➤Take a few minutes to get centered. Focus on the base of your nostrils, where air enters your body, and follow the slow stream of air down into the dark tunnels of your lungs. Become aware of the natural rhythm of your breath.

➤As you expand the interior of your body with the slow and conscious flow of oxygen, stretch your muscles. Stretch the arms to the sides and stretch toward the sky, feeling the stretch in your rib cage and abdomen. Move from side to side, expanding your normal range of movement.

➤When you're ready, sign your name with the wax crayon in an enlarged version to take up the entire sheet. It should not sit inside the page, but push right off the edges. You can sign at an angle or straight up and down. Once you have written your signature, you can enhance it with another color if you like.

➤Turn the large page over now and remove the masking tape or cut through it with a blade along the sheet edges. If you are working with one large sheet, turn it over, measure six equal divisions, and cut it so you will have six sheets.

➤Place the now-separate sheets in front of you in the order in which you had them taped. You're looking at your signature with spaces between it. Study the components of your signature in each segment.

➤Move the sheets around in the six-piece format. Study the lines of your signature when they are pulled away from their normal positions. Play with the order of these pages, exploring new positions, studying new line combinations. The lines now cease to be letters. Continue turning each sheet as you study them individually. When one of them attracts you, go to the next step.

➤Paint and draw on each panel individually. You might want to alternate work, rotating the pieces from time to time. This will give some pieces time to dry, and it will allow you to be working on all of them at once.

➤Remember that you are not painting a picture of any concrete object, but following the linear impulses of your own signature. The outcome will be abstract and colorful. (If you have never painted before, follow the guidelines provided in resource 1.)

➤Continue to work as long as you like. Don't feel you have to finish this in one hour or even in one sitting. You are creating a series of six paintings, so you might prefer to work on them over a period of time.

➤You can do this many times, of course. Each series will be different. Don't get discouraged if you don't like your first attempt. You're using this exercise as a tool to unleash your self-expression and expand your experience of handling paint. It doesn't have to look good or pretty; the importance is in the process and what you're learning from it. You are training your eye and your intellect to accept new possibilities.

Dreams: Unbridled Creativity

Dreams are certainly one of the most fascinating mysteries of the inner well. From dreams of prophecy to mechanical inventions, dreaming has played an important role in human history.

We are aware of being an active recipient in dreaming. We are constantly accepting whatever the dream hands us, feeling the flow of spontaneous and unpredictable images and situations. Though our inner well has created the dream, it seems to have happened to us. We are aware of having very little, if any, control. A student once told me that she considered her dreams to be proof of her creativity. At times when she felt frustrated, she would go back through her journals and read her dreams to reaffirm a sense of creative potential. Dreams are an important component of personal creativity and self-knowledge.

In his empowering book *Dream Work*, Jeremy Taylor writes:

Dreams have long been associated with creative inspiration in the expressive arts, and this popular association has tended to obscure the equally dramatic and consistent history of dream-inspired scientific and technical discovery and innovation. Descartes first formulated the basic philosophical stance of Rational Empiricism which undergirds the entire development of modern science as the result of a vivid dream experience. Kekulé, who was inspired to understand that the molecular structure of benzene is ring-shaped as a result of dreaming of a snake biting its tail, once admonished his colleagues in basic research: "Gentlemen, learn to dream!" Albert Einstein, when asked late in his life just when and where the idea of the Theory of Relativity had first occurred to him, replied that he could not trace the earliest intimations back any further than a dream he had had in adolescence. He recounted that in his dream he was riding on a sled. As the sled accelerated, going faster and faster until it approached the speed of light, the stars began to distort into amazing patterns and colors, dazzling him with the beauty and power of their transformation. He concluded by saying that in many ways, his entire scientific career could be seen as an extended meditation on that dream.*

This historical information about the role of dreams in scientific breakthroughs is important to consider when evaluating the creative power

---

* Jeremy Taylor, *Dream Work: Techniques for Discovering the Creative Power in Dreams* (Ramsey, NJ: Paulist Press, 1983), 7.

of the unconscious mind. Dream messages are largely expressed in images (like Kekulé's snake). The wisdom of those images exceeds the grasp of the linguistically developed portion of the brain until remembering the image brings it into the conscious mind, where spoken language can be used to describe it. Unfortunately, describing a dream doesn't explain it, and the wisdom of the symbols can elude even the most well-read dreamer.

How many times have you wished you had a camera to capture a dream image? Unfortunately no such gizmo exists, so the closest we can come to capturing a dream image is to paint it. It certainly doesn't matter if we catch the exact likeness, because, in fact, there is no exact likeness. The most important thing is the experience of going into the self deeply enough to get in touch with the sense memory of the dream.

Some people swear that they do not dream, but sleep studies have proven that everyone dreams every night. The ability to remember dreams, or to give them conscious expression, can be cultivated without a great deal of special training. You may find that the practice of Creative Meditation has already generated increased dreaming. Just as physical muscles work together, the conscious and unconscious mind nurture and express each other. The new stimulus of creative activity may act as a catalyst for dreaming, daydreaming, fantasizing, and active imagination.

Even if you do not remember your dreams, read through the following Dream Painting process. Ask yourself if it's possible that you forget your dreams. You may be afraid to remember them. It's encouraging to know that psychologists largely agree that dreams come as a tool of healing and wholeness. Try not to be afraid. My experience with Creative Meditation students who begin painting from their most frightening dreams tells me that putting frightening images out into the light takes away some of their threatening power. Making a series of paintings allows those images to evolve as symbols, the language of the unconscious mind. Dream images are icons, and painting them helps to teach us our own unique symbolic language. An increased facility with such a language helps us to see and understand the metaphorical power of the symbols that surround us.*

The dignity of self can never be destructive socially or creatively—it can only enrich the lives and art of both women and men.

SYLVIA STONE

---

* There are many excellent dream books available. *Dream Work* provides a good beginning, because as well as offering an understanding of dream symbolism and process, Taylor also provides both an individual and a group method for approaching dream work.

Exercise:
Dream Painting

Dream images are illusive-feeling pictures. You will not be able to reproduce an image concretely as it appeared, so mood will be an important part of creating a satisfying piece. As you work on your dream paintings, color may become an important tool in achieving the emotional tone you want to express. Be patient, take your time, and if you get frustrated while working on a particular piece, put down the brush and go back to revisit the dream. When you feel reconnected with the dream experience, return to painting.

Supplies

Prepare supplies and work space as for Love Painting II (see page 59).

Process I

The first way to do dream painting is to work alone, painting from your own dreams. If you don't write down your dreams, I suggest you begin to do so. If you don't have a journal, get a special notebook or log just for dreams. Dreams are the only visible part of your unconscious mind, so it's important to begin paying attention to them.

Be patient with yourself. Begin by checking in with how you feel when you wake up, then work backward, remembering the general experience of the night's sleep. If you recall waking up, or a period of restlessness, try to sink back into that feeling in your body. Think into yourself. This may feel foreign to you at first, but approach it as a relaxing meditation. If the images do not become more vivid, simply get into the practice of sinking into the feelings in your body. Gently change body positions, as certain positions may bring back a dream you had in that position.

Let your feelings be your guide to the color or tool with which you begin. Stay focused on the sense memory of the body, and the work will soon find its own direction. Try not to judge yourself as to how well you're doing; you can't do this wrong.

If you're already a dream collector, someone who remembers and records dreams prolifically, you will want to make some choices about which dream(s) to work from. Some dreams are visually very exciting or humorous, while others are very frightening. Painting the images from dreams can make the terrifying manageable, and the seemingly unimportant provocative. The essential purpose of this exercise is creativity enhancement, but a person in psychotherapy can stretch the benefits of dream painting by incorporating it into the therapeutic process.

If you have a specific dream from which you want to work, begin by writing it down; if it's already written, reread it. Ask yourself: What are the major images here, the images that stand out in my mind? Jot them down. Isolate key words. Ask yourself if you want to paint the entire dream as if in a minimural or if you want to paint one specific element. You may want to paint the entire dream in separate sequential pieces.

Since the purpose of this book is to use these images to prime the pump of your creative well, allow yourself total freedom to draw from the basic raw material of the dream. Let me give you an example. Let's say the dream gives you a man in a blue suit who becomes embarrassed because he's late for church. Begin by painting the scene as you perceived it in the dream. Creating that painting may make you aware of other details or parts of the dream that you had forgotten. In the next painting you might expand upon the man's embarrassment and paint the man red instead of flesh tone. This red man in a blue suit might also have numbers written all over his face or cranium to represent the time he's so concerned with. His face could eventually become the face of a clock.

When you work in this way, the dream becomes a catalyst that will continue to stimulate your imagination. Once you have exhausted the image or you feel finished, put the paintings away. Bringing them out in two weeks may evoke an entirely new set of images, ideas, or dreams.

The size of these paintings is not important. You can do them in your journal, or work larger if you like. You may find it helpful to start out working small, getting larger as the images feel stronger or clearer in your mind.

Process II

The second approach to dream painting includes a partner. Each person tells the other a dream. The recipient then writes down the dream and reads it to the dreamer to be sure of details. After agreeing on a time frame, the partners separate and paint the received dream.

Begin with a painting or paintings that remain true to the dream as it was told, then continue, allowing the dream images to grow and change. Do as much work from this dream as possible. If poetry or stories arise, jot them down or speak them into a tape recorder as they develop.

Come together again at the prearranged time and share the fruits of your Creative Meditations. Begin with person A rereading aloud the dream he or she received before sharing the first paintings. Person B then responds, and you have time for discussion. Then person B follows suit, rereading the received dream and sharing the painting(s). Person A has time to respond. Once the original dream work has been discussed, the rest of the work can be shared, beginning with person A.

You and your partner may then decide to get a large piece of paper and create a piece together inspired by the experience, or you may decide to continue the process, perhaps exchanging a particular painting or telling another dream. Among family members this may lead to an open dialogue, or begin to incorporate other people.

Sacred Acts

Coming into a sense of sacred selfhood is akin to taking on a priesthood or ministry. Just as our ancestors celebrated their priesthood through mask making, dancing, drumming, and painting, we are called to interact with the divine on a personal level.

Perhaps you were taught, as I was, that a sacrament was something administered by a priest or minister. Whether or not this concept rings true for you at this time in your life, I present you with the idea that the sacraments are more than those listed by certain institutional canons. A dictionary definition includes "Something considered to have sacred significance; a spiritual symbol or bond."

Love is a sacrament. Beauty is a sacrament. Peace is a sacrament. Creativity is a sacrament. These things course through us just as surely as our blood. These are our sacred bonds with the divine and with each other: they are sacraments administered by the divine through the human. By manifesting these divine energies, we commit sacred acts. Our love may be expressed through charity, compassion, art, or sex. Beauty may be spoken or written, it may be physically pleasing or emotionally stirring. The constant search toward self-fulfillment is in the service of these sacraments, and self-acceptance is an experience of receiving God. The seeker of wisdom and truth asks to become the finest vessel through which such sacraments may pour forth. When considered in this context, creativity is a sacred bond with the divine, so opening ourselves to our own creativity is opening up to God. Creative acts are acts of communion as well as self-expression.

In the next exercise you can incorporate a combination of materials as an act of self-affirmation and expression. It is a way of celebrating communion with yourself. Once all your materials are set up and you're ready to begin, reread the above passage on sacred acts and sacraments. While working, think about yourself, your birth, your life, and your whole existence within that context.

In my opinion all important things in art . . . have always originated from the deepest feeling about the mystery of Being. Self-realization is the urge of all objective spirits. It is this self which I am searching for in my life and in my art.

MAX BECKMANN

Exercise:
Self-Portrait

The self-portrait is a traditional form in painting. Perhaps more than any other painter, Rembrandt van Rijn, the great Dutch master, used this form throughout his life to explore and express himself with sometimes painful honesty. Unlike the traditional format, however, this self-portrait will not require you to capture your own physical likeness.

This process is geared to self-exploration as well as expression. It's an especially good way to look at where you are and where you have been in your life. If you are going through a transition (divorce, illness, or career change, for example), this will be a useful tool for analyzing and celebrating the course of your life. If you have not yet come to recognize your gracefulness, this project should help. I suggest allowing several weeks for developing and executing it.

Part I

This project can be done in many ways. The supplies listed are suggestions; you are completely free to embellish upon these suggestions. If you want to work on canvas or fabric, for example, go ahead with your own ideas.

Supplies

* A piece of butcher paper two feet longer than your height
* Masking tape
* A soft lead pencil and kneaded eraser
* A black felt-tip pen
* A helper (needed only for about fifteen minutes)

Getting to Work

➤Roll the butcher paper out on the floor. (This works best if you are not on a carpet.) Tape the paper lightly at the four corners. Lie down on it and move around for a while. The physically challenged reader may want to tape the butcher paper to a wall. Decide what type of posture or stance you would like for the outline of your body. The stance you choose can say a lot about the way you portray yourself.

➤ Once you have chosen your stance, stretch out very still on the paper. Have your helper trace your body onto the butcher paper with the pencil. The person drawing the outline should keep in mind that she or he is drawing a person, not just blindly following a form. Though you can make corrections later, attention to details and proportions should be considered. With the pencil drawing finished to your satisfaction, go over it with a black felt marker (unless you plan to paint it without using heavy lines).

➤ Once the outline is finished, find a wall where you can hang it.

➤ Study this outline of yourself for several days. When you feel ready, sit down with the following reflection questions:

- Name the blessings of your life. What parts of yourself can you name and celebrate freely? What parts of yourself are you reluctant to claim? (Do not leave out your body. These questions refer to all aspects of your life.)

- What things do you work at, and what comes easily to you?

- Reflect on your dark side. What don't you like about yourself? What things have brought you pain? What are you afraid of?

- What is your relationship to work (to work in general as well as your specific work)? To play? Do you have an avocation? What part does it play in your life?

- Is there a song that best describes your philosophy of life? Can its lyrics or images become a part of your self-portrait?

- Reflecting on your psychological/spiritual evolution, can you describe where you have been? Where are you going? What conflicts you are dealing with?

- What do you love? Whom do you love? How do you love?

- What are your dreams or visions for the future, and how much attention do you pay to them?

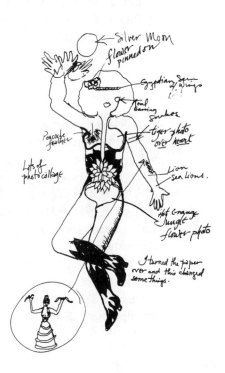

Part II

Once you have answered the above questions and are ready to reflect the answers on this butcher paper mirror, you are ready to begin the next phase. This self-portrait will be a self-representation. That is to say, it need not be a likeness of you. You may decide to paint it, or paint parts of it. You may decide to collage a part of it, or all of it. I usually encourage an eclectic approach to represent the many facets of the personality and the diversity of one's feelings.

Supplies

You may use anything. Consider the following as suggestions.
* Water-based paints
* Felt markers (Remember that most of these fade; indelible markers are available but are more expensive. Check with your art supplier.)
* Rubber cement, scissors, brushes of various sizes, water containers, old magazines, newspapers, fabric remnants, old pieces of jewelry (lightweight things can be sewn or glued on)

Getting to Work

Give yourself ample work periods (at least an hour at a time), and if possible keep the self-portrait out where you can see it between work sessions. Looking at it frequently will give you new ideas, and will probably elicit conversation from those who see it taking shape. How will you deal with such witnesses? Recognizing that this can be a very personal experience, try to be as receptive to comments as possible, but do not feel any responsibility to share the intimacies of your personal process. You might want to keep this book nearby, and when someone asks what you're doing turn to this section, and let them read about the project.

Above all try to listen with an open mind, not in the name of good manners, but for the sake of future work. Once you begin painting a lot, you will realize that every piece feels like a self-portrait to a certain extent. Receiving comments or critiques is an important talent to develop, and can be educational.

Part III

When the self-portrait is finished, hang it on the wall near your altar, if possible. Take some time to close your eyes and mentally relive your experience of making this piece. Ask yourself if your creative and technical process parallels your life process. For example: Do you usually have trouble getting started on a project and gain speed and enthusiasm once you've clarified your ideas? Do you keep changing and shifting the concept of what you're trying to achieve? Did you go through characteristic mood swings while working on the project? Do you tend to leave things unfinished? Is that the case with this project as well? Did you approach it with a sense of fun or one of drudgery? Did your enthusiasm wane? What caused that waning?

Part IV

Finish the following in fifteen minutes. (You need not use a timer, but staying in the fifteen-minute time frame will help you to come up with something quickly.)

➤Establish a new name for this portrait, in the tradition of Native American naming. Names such as Hearty Earth Sister or Soaring Eagle come from within the heart and soul of a person; they tell us something about that person's character. Allow your new name to surface as a process of meditation.

Once you are relaxed and at rest deep within yourself, bring forth all the things you have learned about yourself. Let an integrating image come to mind. This image will bring your name.

➤Writing in the third person, create a brief statement about this person. The statement should tell what kind of person this is; where he or she is headed in life; and perhaps what the person's basic philosophy is.

➤Design a small ritual to celebrate your self. If you are celebrating alone, you may want to take a photo of your self-portrait so that you can enact your ritual at the beach or on top of a mountain. You may want to include friends and family. If you have recently accomplished a major goal or survived a difficult ordeal, this ritual can be a powerful act of self-affirmation.

CHAPTER THREE

The Reverential Eye: Seeing as the Essence of Creative Communion

*L*EARNING TO DRAW was probably the most significant step in my spiritual awakening. The story of my experience as a young college student (see the Introduction) is the account of a young woman's initiation into the sacred and loving nature of the universe. Years of religious study and prayer had not been able to give me the experience of communion with the world that drawing did. Drawing taught me not only to have trust in that which I could not see, but also to trust and have reverence for the fully visible world around me.

Drawing is a practice of being intimately receptive and in communion with our environment. Through drawing as meditation we develop the reverential eye that sees the sacred beauty of all things. It can teach you to understand the difference between knowing about something, seeing something, and really knowing something.

Drawing will develop a cooperative process between your mind and your eyes. The mind must relinquish the role of know-it-all; it must allow the eye to be the teacher. The mind makes a lot of assumptions. Most of the time these assumptions are close enough to reality that we can get along in the world. In drawing, however, the less you assume the more you will see. The painter's eye is one that presumes ignorance and is therefore always delighted with discoveries.

As each person expands the ability to see, imagine, and envision, the culture becomes more capable of meeting the challenges of the present and the future in creative and original ways. Seeing the magnificence of the external world helps us discover and accept the mysteries of the inner world. Painting from a dream is equal to painting from a sunset. I am convinced that seeing with the reverential eye, a painter's eye, can guide this planet into a future of innovation and compassion.

Artistic vision is the ability to see into and beyond the visible surface. This is the gift the artist brings to society. It is a cultivated sight that develops from the spiritual discipline of looking at the world. There are actually two stages in the cultivation of this vision. The first has to do with learning to see: the power to see honestly what is physically present. The second stage is about developing vision from sight. Visioning is the power to conjure and create new things, things that have never before been seen or heard. This is a magical power that can be ours when we receive the universe as our inspiration.

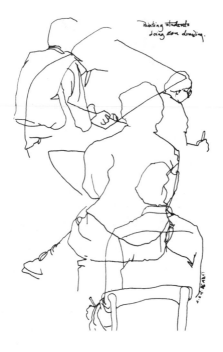

One day, after a drawing exercise, one of my students said in amazement, "Every time I draw something I fall in love!" I wasn't surprised to hear this, because I know that when we wake up to the world around us in full form, with vivid colors, lines, and shapes, we become filled with awe and wonder. It is easy to fall in love with the things we've walked past so many times, because we realize that the world is offering itself to us like a lover longing for our embrace and recognition. Receiving the universe in all its diversity allows us a new self-appreciation, and coming to a level of self-acceptance and self-love prepares us to love the world in return. When this awareness lives at our core, celebration becomes a way of life. We recognize and accept each person in her or his own psychic, spiritual, and physical form. Oppression of self and others has no place in such a mindset, and compassion becomes the foundation for all behavior.

Maturity of Perception

In listening to student dialogues about works of art, I observed that nearly everyone began by passing judgment. Phrases such as "I like this because . . ." or "I don't like this painting" preceded any other comments. I realized that this initial way of responding was indicative of the judgmental approach students brought to their own work.

We learn in elementary school to incorporate judging with doing. If you're like me, a little voice in your head usually accompanies every activity. Its monologue goes a bit like this: "Oh, boy, this is great. What fun! . . . Oh, no, I don't like that. . . . That's no good, maybe this will fix it. . . . Oh, yuk! That's terrible. Better try another. . . . Oh, great, that's better . . . now it looks really good. I could put more over here. . . . Oh, no! . . . You ruined it, Stupid. I hope nobody sees this. Oh God, I can't do this stuff . . . "

And so it goes on, ad nauseum!

I have learned that what I have not drawn I have never truly seen, and that when I start drawing an ordinary thing I realize how extraordinary it is, sheer miracle.

FREDERICK FRANCK

The painter draws with his eyes, not with his hands. Whatever he sees, if he sees it clear, he can put down.

MAURICE GROSSER

We are taught to judge ourselves by the constant judgment that we experience as children. We're surrounded by authorities who teach us to be critical of ourselves by the way they treat us. We learn to anticipate the judgment of others, and we try to fend off external criticism by being the first to judge our own behavior and work.

Self-criticism is a learned behavior, and it can be unlearned. Judgment can be turned into constructive evaluation. Daring to live a more creative life will help you to establish your own framework for evaluation. This is an enormous step in self-empowerment. Above all, you will learn to give yourself permission to take greater creative risks in every aspect of your life.

Welcoming your creativity through Creative Meditation is a way to wake up to a new perception, a more mature perception than you have ever known. You've already developed this maturity of perception in other areas. Let me give you an example. Read the following excerpt from a poem by Adrienne Rich.

> If I cling to circumstances I could feel
> not responsible. Only she who says
> she did not choose, is the loser in the end.*

As an adolescent you may not have understood the richness of these lines. As an adult you can taste the full flavor of each word. The poem is rich with emotion, the emotions you share with the poet. You are at a time in your life when you have the maturity of perception that allows you to understand the unspoken dimensions of this poetry. The poet speaks the words, the words of your experience, and your perception and memory allow you to take part in the poem.

Drawing

Drawing as a spiritual practice is an involvement of the entire self. Just as in the poetry example above, in which we celebrate a communion with the poet, through drawing we celebrate communion with the subject.

The work we did earlier to clear away the childhood obstructions that have kept you from this form of communion now begins to provide an avenue for this new experience. Drawing and painting require mental and spiritual preparation. The ceremonies and painting experiences you have

---

* Adrienne Rich, *The Dream of a Common Language: Poems 1974–77* (New York: Norton, 1978), 33.

already done are a part of your preparation. You are already a different person than you were when you began.

To understand what drawing/seeing is about, it's helpful to examine our use of the verb *to draw*. One might say: "I was very drawn to that person," or "Mary was very withdrawn at the party," or "I had blood drawn." In each of these cases we understand a slow pull of energy. We are drawn to people who seem to have a magnetism about them. When we are feeling badly, we retreat physically, emotionally, or spiritually.

So what does this have to do with seeing, or drawing on paper? The type of drawing presented in this book is a method of recording an experience of being drawn into the presence of another. When I do this drawing meditation, I do not begin the drawing with my pencil. I begin in my soul. I invite the chosen subject of my work to enter my life. In turn, I ask it to open up to me, inviting me into its home. This is a great honor and should be done with respect.

Outside of the handshake, or intrafamilial greeting customs, American culture does not have inherent ceremonies by which we honor each other's presence, as in the Japanese custom of bowing, for example. Consequently, we do not develop a mind-set for valuing the spiritual presence of relatives, colleagues, friends, or neighbors. Growing up in a Hispanic tradition, I have always been accustomed to considerably more formality in this regard. For instance, it is customary when entering the home of a respected acquaintance to wait to be invited in, prefacing one's entrance with the phrase *"con su permiso"* ("with your permission"). This custom is especially fitting in developing drawing as a spiritual practice, because it pays respect to the space in which another being resides, as well as acknowledging the trust with which others allow us into their sphere.

After I have opened my soul to the subject I have chosen, I engage my eye. At this point, Seeing begins. This capital-S seeing indicates the kind of Sight from which wisdom is born. I may have looked at my subject a million times, I may know its name as well as my own, but I may not have Seen it. Seeing is intimate; it is a walk along the surface of my subject's body with an awe-filled eye and an empty head.

To create is always to learn, to begin over, to begin at zero. Part of the discipline of art as meditation is the discipline of struggling always from the beginning.

MATTHEW FOX

Becoming Empty-Headed

An empty head is very important and very difficult to attain. As I said earlier, the mind must sit in the backseat and let the eyes be in charge. In the discipline of drawing meditation, I'm asking my subject to fill my space with its story. I ask to be taught.

I remember one vivid winter's day at Versailles. Silence and calm reigned supreme. Everything gazed at me with mysterious, questioning eyes. And then I realized that every corner of the palace, every column, every window possessed a spirit, an impenetrable soul. I looked around at the marble heroes, motionless in the lucid air, beneath the frozen rays of that winter sun which pours down on us without love, like perfect song. A bird warbling in a window cage. At that moment I grew aware of the mystery which urges men to create certain strange forms. And the creation appeared more extraordinary than the creators.

GIORGIO DE CHIRICO

This is conscious empty-headedness, which means that we become aware of our ignorance and enjoy it. We welcome it as a vast inner void ready to receive what the Chinese refer to as the Ten Thousand Things. The Buddhists refer to this inner space as No Mind, a state to be attained through meditation practice. One allows all thought to clear away, leaving a space of pure existence. In drawing meditation the mind is simply made a hospitable space for the subject to enter. It's important to clear the space of intellectual assumptions that keep the eye from Seeing clearly and honestly.

This type of seeing is an intentional personal engagement. It is an act of spiritual intimacy, a more profound interaction with the world than most of us have ever known. Learning to see and to know communion with creatures, things, and other people can liberate us from the imprisonment of alienation on a personal and global level. When we see ourselves as separate creatures fighting for survival, we devour animals, trees, water, even space without concern or awareness of our effect. The experience of drawing meditation suddenly awakens the eye and the mind to the sacred vitality of the Earth and our connection to all its life forms. This is a truly transformative and sacred experience, and I would encourage those of you who have children to involve the whole family in this meditation practice once you are comfortable with it on your own.

Moving Beyond Labels

If I draw my mother's face, I must let go of everything I "know" about her. When I let go of the idea of drawing that entity that I know so well as Mother, then I can receive what her face has to tell me. Her eyes, nose, and mouth can tell me about themselves. Only they can tell me about their shape, their lines. Though I have looked at my mother since childhood, she is unknown to me until I have Seen her. Close your eyes for a moment and try to see the shape of your mother's lips. Can you see how they change when she smiles?

It's easy to get caught up in the mythology of objects. Below is a list of some household objects that you could easily recognize if they were set in front of you. See if you can create an image of these items in your mind's eye. Close your eyes between each item on the list. (Better still, have someone slowly read the list to you so you can just relax and visualize.)

Manual can opener
Bottle opener

Butter knife
Hammer
Safety razor
Screwdriver

In your painting journal, draw the objects that you can image most clearly in your mind. Please don't take this exercise too seriously. I am hoping you will be able to feel the difference between this type of playful drawing and the spiritual experience of drawing meditation.

This list of labels probably activated some types of images. Whether or not you were able to visualize them clearly, you're probably confident of your ability to recognize objects such as can openers or safety razors. These images, however, are exactly the ones you must clear from your mind before drawing. They are cliché images that make up an easy-reference visual vocabulary. While they're of great help when cartooning or doodling, when you get into drawing meditation these stereotypical images inhibit you from honestly Seeing what is in front of you.

Labels give superficial information, a code for easy filing. In this fast-paced world we recognize this labeling system as a natural survival technique. Few of us can afford the time to look at each person or thing with intense honesty and appreciation. But I suggest that (after you've done the basic two sessions) if you spend a minimum of ten minutes a day doing drawing meditation you will naturally begin to see more of everything around you.

A New Frame for Time

Just as rests are a vital part of music, moments of stillness are as dynamic as moments of activity in painting. In the concentrated breathing and meditations we have already done, we've realized that in those still spaces we touch a profound depth of self, we contact ancestral energy, and we find our dormant creative spirit. We have a deep desire to participate in Creation, and as we accept the invitation of that desire, as we dip brush into paint, a silent rhythm begins to hum deep within. With the first stroke of color our creative dance is set in motion, and we are spontaneously responding to the movement of the paint. A painting takes form moment by moment, shifting, changing, and growing.

Artist and teacher Frederick Franck has addressed this phenomenon as it applies to the art of Seeing in one of his masterfully written books, *The Awakened Eye* (companion book to *The Zen of Seeing*). Franck gives us

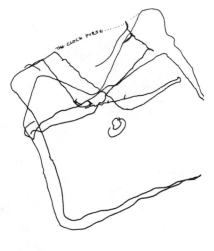

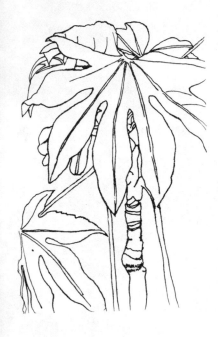

the Eastern perspective of prayer through drawing. In addressing the issue of time he quotes the *Hwa Yen Sutra:* "The incalculable eons are but one moment, and this moment is no moment."

> The 7th century masters had become aware of time as composed of ultra-short time fragments which they called NEN, thought-moments of such flashing brevity that for all practical purposes they could be called timeless.*

Franck goes on to explain that a first NEN moment is the first instant of immediate experience of the eye on a subject. "When my eye perceives something in the outer world, it registers it during the first, immeasurably short mini-instant or NEN, in a direct vision which is purely intuitive and cognitive, as in a flash of profound insight into that which is seen." This first NEN moment is your body's excitement. It is the instant of life evoking life. The optic nerve experiences excitement without judgment, because our bodies are hungry for the dance of creation and are poised for action. Nerves and muscles respond in a split second; they don't ask for permission, they don't wait for opinions.

Get out a piece of paper and the brilliant water colors you used for the Breath of God exercise. Blow a color around on the page. Feel your eyes widening and moving with the paint. Think back to your experience of the Breath of God exercise. The vibrancy of the colors on the white surface is always a joyful stimulation to the eye. You can feel the ongoing ecstatic encounter of that first NEN moment.

What immediately follows, according to Franck, is a "second NEN" and a "third NEN."

> The second NEN is a flash of mental reflection, of becoming aware of my intuitive insight, of this profound "knowing." But in the "third NEN," which follows just as rapidly, this awareness becomes "my" awareness: both previous flashes become integrated in my continuous stream of consciousness; are processed as it were, in that region of the mind where reasoning, labeling, introspection— in short, ego feeling take over. The experience now becomes part of "my" consciousness and at once the Me begins to interpret, to rationalize and to draw "logical" conclusions from the direct perception, to distort the direct, "clairvoyant" grasp of the first NEN, and to imprison it once more in words and concepts. These cogitations,

---

* Frederick Franck, *The Awakened Eye* (New York: Vintage Books, 1979), 104.

analyses and conclusions snowball further until the intuitive revelation of the first NEN is totally lost.*

Contemplating this NEN sequence, it is easy to see where the meditational and prayerful dimension of creativity can break down. By the time our organism is into that third NEN mode, we are filled with self and devoid of awe. Awe is reverent presence and attentiveness; it is the essence of the prayerful dimension of Creative Meditation.

Whereas Zen meditation practice moves toward selflessness, that is, toward an emptying of self, a state of No Mind, Creative Meditation calls on you to be more fully present in your nonrational mind. The third NEN is impossible to stop, but its transformation into a stage of creativity is essential to this process.

Let's reread Franck's description:

The experience now becomes part of "my" consciousness and at once the Me begins to interpret, to rationalize and to draw "logical" conclusions from the direct perception, to distort the direct, "clairvoyant" grasp of the first NEN.

What I'd like you to see here is this: the first NEN is your natural, intuitive response. It is nonlinear, noncausal, nonrational. Trust this part of yourself. The more you trust that first NEN grasp of the universe, the more you will be able to relax into your connection to and reverence for life. Beginning artists have a great desire to prove control of the medium, but Creative Meditation frees you from that impulse when you embrace creativity as a spiritual practice. This is worship: there is nothing to prove and nothing to control.

When I first read Dr. Franck's section on the third NEN stage of labeling and judging, I immediately recognized my own process. "Darn me," I cursed, "I shouldn't do that. How can I stop doing that?" I got terribly frustrated with myself until I realized I was doing that self-judging thing again. Rather than continuing to admonish myself, I tried to release myself from the old training. I gave myself permission to do what came naturally, NEN by NEN.

The following exercise (drawing 1) (like finger painting and straw blowing) is helpful for developing the moment-to-moment first NEN awareness. Do these kinds of processes as often as you like to stretch and free up your physical and psychological muscles. Try to maintain a NEN by NEN consciousness in order to keep yourself from becoming intellectually judgmental of your creative process.

It is looking at things for a long time that ripens you and gives you a deeper understanding. If we study Japanese art, we see an artist who is wise, philosophic, and intelligent, who spends his time—how? He studies a single blade of grass. But this blade of grass leads him to draw the plant, and then the season, the wide aspects of the countryside, the animals, then the human figures. So he passes his life.

Come, now, isn't it almost an actual religion which these simple Japanese teach us, who live in nature as though they themselves were flowers? We must return to nature in spite of our education and our work in a world of convention. And you cannot study Japanese art without becoming gayer and happier.

VINCENT VAN GOGH

---

* Ibid., 105.

The Possibility of Failure

There are three things that can keep you from progressing and improving with this drawing process: rushing, trying to create drawings as a product, and not practicing. Don't try to imitate art. Treat these brief meditations as minivacations, a chance to enter a new world. You will be welcomed into the world of your subject, and you will find each experience a fascinating, spiritual, and educational adventure.

Despite the frustrations you may feel from time to time, please do not chide yourself. If your drawing meditation is prayerful, then it will be successful in teaching you reverence for life on both its greater and more diminutive scale.

Preparatory Reflection

I'd like you to take some time going back into your experience as a child before limitations were placed on you. Put on some meditative music; lie or sit comfortably in a safe and quiet space. Try to relive the keen curiosity of your child eyes. Can you remember your favorite things to draw? Did you make any great discoveries about things? Let this feeling of childhood sink into your body. When you feel finished with these memories, release them slowly into the air and return to the room.

Childhood memories can provide the relaxation we need as adults to enjoy the less rational activities of creative play. If you get positive results from this process, spend a little time before each session of play checking in with that courageous kid in you who loved to explore new things. Don't belittle the child hidden deep beneath your adulthood. There is a rich treasure hidden in that youthful foundation; this is your opportunity to retrieve some of your own forgotten wisdom.

The artist is a receptacle for emotions that come from all over the place: from the sky, from the earth, from a scrap of paper, from a passing shape, from a spider's web. That is why we must not discriminate between things. Where things are concerned there are no class distinctions.

PABLO PICASSO

Exercise:
Drawing Meditation Session 1

Allow at least an hour and a half for this first drawing meditation session, and please read through the instructions completely before beginning your first drawing. Also, work in a place that is quiet and undisturbed by phones, family, traffic, or other sounds.

Preparation

I suggest that before beginning you take some time to light a candle and a bit of sage or a stick of incense. A complete ritual is not necessary, but once all the tools are assembled, a moment of centering is very helpful. It will help you to remember the ritual of the Yoruba blessing. You may want to do the blessing again with a small bowl of water nearby. Restate the affirmation about your commitment to letting go of old self-images in order to embrace new possibilities. Give yourself a hospitable inner space in which to learn something new without a litany of critical remarks.

Supplies

* A pad of newsprint paper
* A 2B graphite drawing pencil (do not use any type of felt-tip pen for early drawings, because anywhere you stop, the ink will make a blotch on the newsprint)
* A pencil sharpener (use as needed—you don't need a very sharp point unless you prefer it)
* An audible kitchen timer

* Optional: a drawing board or a cutting board turned over on the smooth side (use this if you cannot find a smooth surface to draw on, or if you prefer to work on a surface that has a bit of a slant)
* Please notice that an eraser is not on this list. Do not have an eraser available.

How to Proceed

Clear your desk or table of all other objects or paraphernalia. Be sure that the surface you're drawing on is free of scratches, knots, or dents.

The absence of an eraser is very important. Mistakes are not an issue here. The absence of the eraser also emphasizes the importance of silencing the inner critic. There's no judgment attached to this process. This form of drawing is not done in order to make something for others to ooh and aah over; you're not doing this drawing process to please anyone. Your first objective is to become what Frederick Franck calls "all eyes."

Drawing #1

➢Crumple a piece of scratch paper (used typing paper or junk mail). This will be your first subject. I like beginning with crumpled paper as a drawing subject, because it's impossible to label and assume things about it. There's no way to draw it without looking at it.

➢Before you begin this first drawing encounter, take a few minutes to relax your body and mind by using the following meditation. You may want to make a cassette of this guided meditation so that you can simply close your eyes and follow the instructions in a more relaxed way.

➢With only your newsprint, pencil, sharpener, and crumpled paper in front of you, sit at a table or desk in a supportive chair with your feet touching the floor. Leave the pencil on the table.

Guided Body Relaxation

As before, the markings ➢➢ and ➢➢➢➢ are provided for pauses in the recording. (Remember to speak slowly when recording.) When you are ready to begin and have read through all the instructions for Drawing #1, close your eyes and play the tape.

Take a deep breath, feeling your abdomen expand as your lungs fill. Slowly exhale. Allow your breathing to flow into a slow and relaxed rhythm, without forcing it into a pattern. On the next inhalation, flare your nostrils. Many animals do this at moments of peak excitement or just before taking action. Flaring your nostrils will help you become focused on the oxygen entering your body.

As you continue breathing deeply, shift your focus to the top of your head. Feel a warm sense of relaxation melt down the back of your head and onto your shoulders. If you feel tension in your neck or shoulders, release it as you exhale. ⊁⊁⊁⊁ Concentrate your breathing into the part or parts of your body where tension still persists. ⊁⊁⊁⊁ Slowly proceed down your back, sensing a feeling of warmth as the relaxation soothes your back muscles. Sit comfortably erect to avoid slouching, which can constrict your lungs and diaphragm. ⊁⊁⊁⊁

When your focus has traveled down the back muscles and spine to your waist, bring it around to your chest and abdomen, still breathing deeply. Your mind and body are growing calm and receptive, and rather than feeling sleepy with this level of relaxation, you will be alert and open to your subject. ⊁⊁⊁⊁ Breathe deeply with a conscious sense of this growing receptivity.

Allow your focus to drop down to the base of your spine and the buttocks muscles. Feel them supporting you. ⊁⊁⊁⊁ Feel the surface contact beneath you. ⊁⊁⊁⊁ Take your attention down into the thighs and calves, ⊁⊁⊁⊁ and finally, into your feet. Feel the point of contact with the floor. ⊁⊁⊁⊁

Now with your eyes closed, relax into a dark, inviting space in the center of your body. ⊁⊁ Stay there for a moment, allowing any images to pass, letting go of each one until you have a calm darkness behind your eyes. ⊁⊁

When you have done that, open your eyes, allowing them to be filled with the crumpled paper before you. Let your eyes stay in one spot on the paper at first, and then begin to travel slowly along the paper's edges and lines. ⊁⊁ Think of becoming an ant slowly strolling along the contours of this vast paper world. ⊁⊁ Do not pick up your pencil or draw anything yet. You are solely interested in knowing this new environment. You have never seen this place before; enjoy its beautiful surface, shapes, and lines.

[Leave a three-minute pause in the tape, then start recording again:]

Close your eyes again, and see the paper in your mind's eye. ⊁⊁⊁⊁ Can you follow the lines as you did with your eyes open? ⊁⊁ Try to bring them into view as much as possible. Spend two minutes reseeing the paper with eyes closed. [Two-minute pause on tape.] Open your eyes and again allow your gaze to land on one spot on the crumpled paper. ⊁⊁ Ask a silent permission to enter the intimate spaces of the paper. Ask it to welcome you. ⊁⊁⊁⊁

When you feel recognition, pick up your pencil and allow it to become the recorder of your interaction with this object. Do not presume anything; allow the crumpled paper to teach you about itself as a person would in conversation. During this drawing do not look down at the image you are creating with your pencil, and do not lift the pencil from the page.

[Leave a five-minute pause here, or set a timer. End the exercise with a simple instruction, such as the following:]

Close your eyes now, set down the pencil, and come to rest.

There are a number of reasons for this final instruction regarding looking at the drawing and lifting the pencil. First, if you have great expectations of yourself, these restrictions will free you from having to fulfill them. Second, you can give yourself permission to focus only on Seeing. Third, the restrictions free you from the responsibility of the final outcome, helping you to let go of the natural desire to be in control of the image. If you hear a critical voice in your head as you are working, send it away by reminding it that you are too busy learning about the object and cannot look away.

➤Continue this drawing encounter for five minutes. (Again, a timer can be very helpful to free you from keeping track of the time.) At the end of the drawing, you will be anxious to see what it looks like. If you have used a pencil with a hard lead, the lines will be very light. Get a softer lead pencil, as suggested in the instructions. It will give a stronger image without a great deal of tension in the hand or pressure on the page.

➤Please don't try to evaluate your drawing. Whatever you did is great. The important thing is the process. It's natural to want to achieve something, but keep in mind that the drawing you just did was a meditation. The only question I would ask you is: Did you See the crumpled paper? You may want to spend a little time reflecting on the experience. You may decide to keep written reflections in your painting journal.

➤Number your first drawing as #1, and do another one following the same instructions. (I suggest you use the same sheet of paper. You can even work on the same side as #1.) Toss the crumpled paper into the air and allow it to fall into a new position.

➤Use the same breathing and centering preparation, though you need not go through the entire body meditation unless you want to. Simply close your eyes and go into a dark inner space. Some areas of tension may reveal themselves as you slowly let the breath go deeper. Again, exhale the tension and gently stretch any places that feel stiff or tense.

➤Do the next drawing at half the speed of the first one. I have never seen anyone go too slowly (which I would define as "stopped"). Our eyes are not accustomed to Seeing. We usually dash across objects with lightning speed. In this drawing process, you're attempting to coordinate the pencil and the eye. They should eventually move together, synchronized in a slow process of Seeing and recording what is seen.

Pacing is one of the most important factors in any of the Creative Meditation projects. My normal life pace is so fast that each time I begin painting or drawing I must make a conscious effort to slow my internal rhythm before I can slow my hands. Creative Meditation has been my salvation from hours of frustration. Let yourself sink into this process, and return to it whenever you need to focus and slow down.

Give yourself permission to take an occasional hour (or more) with nothing to show for it. Think in terms of resetting an inner metronome. (You might consider using a real metronome for assistance.) You may want to add some soothing music; simple flute music works very well. Surrender to tranquillity. Take a vacation from yourself and your problems. A positive side effect of a meditative break is that when you're finished, you'll be more clearheaded and creative about tackling pressing issues and making decisions.

Drawings #2 and #3

➤Do several five- to seven-minute drawings of the crumpled paper, with a breathing and centering process between the drawings. Be sure to number each drawing as you finish it. It's not unusual for people to experience eye fatigue doing this drawing meditation, because we seldom really take the time to look at anything with this intensity or for this length of time. Give your eyes frequent rest periods. In fact, after you have done four drawings, leave your work space for a bit. Take fifteen minutes for a short walk, stretch, or drink of water. The break will help you notice your increased level of awareness when you begin the next meditation.

➤After you have meditated for an hour and a quarter, reflect back to your beginning experience. Look at Drawing #1 and reflect on how you felt during that drawing.

➤Ask yourself the following questions:

- When did I really See this thing?
- When did I feel seen or welcomed?
- What's my biggest obstacle to feeling comfortable with this process?

➤If you are hearing a critical voice while you're meditating, try to determine the source of it. Is it from a particular person, or a singular traumatic experience? Are you still trying to impress someone? If so, why? If it won't go away, talk to it, ask it what it wants from you. Then tell it to get lost.

I cannot be emphatic enough about the importance of practice when it comes to improving drawing technique. Hopefully, before going on to session 2, you'll spend time doing drawing meditation with various objects without looking at the page and without lifting the pencil. This is extremely important, because it establishes the ability to see and connect.

Selecting Objects to Draw

You'll find that simple objects work best for drawing meditation. Because you're beginning to see so much more than you ever have, you know that even simple objects can be overwhelming to the eye. Clean lines that are clearly visible are best. Stay away from furry objects, or things with quills or needles. Leaves, flowers, and bare branches are great, but don't feel you have to draw the entire object at one sitting. Stay away from globular or very smooth objects like bowls, vases, or glassware. Sections of fabric are excellent subjects, especially fabrics that undulate and fold in distinct shapes with well-defined edges.

Exercise: Drawing Meditation
Session 2—Exterior/Interior

The next adventure in Seeing explores an object while using it as a tool for personal discovery. You will need the same supplies as for session 1, plus an object that can reveal an interior. This may be, for example, a small box, a locket, an apple, or a pistachio. (Don't choose a walnut—it's far too complex inside.) Take my advice: keep it simple. Don't use your tool box or your purse full of goodies. You will be greatly relieved to keep it simple, because when you really See it, even the least complex object will be far more intricate than you ever realized.

Preparation

Before going into the project itself, I'd like to share with you something from the life and work of the great German poet Rainer Maria Rilke. Rilke was fascinated by the art of painting. He spent a great deal of time living in a painters' colony, and letters written to his wife during a stay in Paris tell of his devotion to the work of the French painter Paul Cézanne. In the following excerpt from *News of the Universe,* Robert Bly tells of the lessons Rilke learned while employed by the great sculptor August Rodin.

> Rilke was Rodin's secretary for a while, and Rodin one day advised him to go down to the zoo and try to see something. Rilke did, and spent some time watching a panther. Rodin respected seeing, the ability to observe, to use the terrific energy of the eyes, to pay attention to something besides one's own subjectivity. Rilke understood that his own poetry lacked seeing, and he wrote nearly two hundred poems in about six years in an effort to sharpen his seeing. Through that labor, Rilke passed to a new stage of his art.*

It is important to realize that this quest for sight has played an essential role in the works of great artists of all forms. The composer must first see through all his or her senses before guiding us to see through our ears. The poet puts into language that which we often perceive only through intuition. Below is the poem that Rilke wrote about the panther he saw at the zoo. The intensity with which the poet eventually saw the animal is evident in the final work. He reached such a level of communion with the panther that the poem reveals both the interior condition of the animal and his external situation; the two, poet and subject, seem merged into a singular voice.

---

* Bly, *News of the Universe,* 210.

THE PANTHER

In the Jardin des Plantes, Paris

From seeing the bars, his seeing is so exhausted
that it no longer holds anything anymore.
To him the world is bars, a hundred thousand
bars, and behind the bars, nothing.

The lithe swinging of that rhythmical easy stride
which circles down to the tiniest hub
is like a dance of energy around a point
in which a great will stands stunned and numb.

Only at times the curtains of the pupil rise
without a sound . . . then a shape enters,
slips through the tightened silence of the shoulders,
reaches the heart, and dies.*

The drawings done through this method of drawing meditation are like the poems that came from Rilke's seeing/writing experiences. They are exercises in getting out of your own way, of pushing beyond the enclosure of the human ego into the lively world of others—especially the silent ones with whom we have so little other communication.

The outcome of such a seeing experience is not only effective on the artistic level, but enormously moving on the spiritual level. Ancient religions of Eastern and Western traditions have long recognized the presence of divine energy in all things. Drawing meditation will give you a firsthand understanding of Buddha nature, the Tao, grace, and what Meister Eckhart referred to as "isness."

Getting to Work

In this exercise, I have included a time for questioning and personal reflection on the nature of your own face. We can see a reflection of Rilke through his opening line about the panther: his concern with seeing, and his exhaustion. We even get a sense of time elongated by imprisonment. If you haven't had an opportunity to practice since doing Drawing Meditation Session 1, I suggest that you go back over the instructions for that exercise. You will be using the same format for preparation and meditation in this exercise.

---

* *Selected Poems of Rainer Maria Rilke*, trans. Robert Bly (New York: Harper & Row, 1981), 139.

➢When you've selected the article you'll be working with, set up your drawing space as before (see Drawing Meditation Session 1) with timer, paper, pencil, and sharpener. Clear away everything else. Place the timer in a spot where you can depress it after your meditation without taking your eyes off the subject. Set it for a seven-minute drawing. Play some soft music if you wish. You'll be doing several drawings, which you may want to put on one sheet of paper. Often, three different views of the same object in one drawing creates an interesting composition.

➢Place the object in front of you in its closed position—that is, with only its exterior revealed.

➢Close your eyes and go through the body relaxation meditation outlined in Drawing Meditation Session 1. (You can see that it is very helpful to have that meditation on tape so that you can use it whenever you need it.) When you feel relaxed and emptied of all other images, connect with the object you have chosen. Think about how you selected this object. Think about the object as you have seen it so far. What label do you have for it? What kind of feelings do you have about it? As a way of opening a field of receptivity between you and your subject, remember the Spanish custom (*"con su permiso"*), and ask permission to enter its intimate space. Then with open heart and cleared vision, open your eyes, allowing your gaze to fall on one spot on the object's surface.

➢Keeping your eyes and hand moving at a slow and coordinated pace, allow the pencil to record the experience of your eye caressing the lines of your subject. If you have been practicing, you may feel confident about looking down at the page from time to time. Introduce this slowly, keeping it to a minimum at first, increasing it as you develop stronger concentration.

The danger in looking down at the page is the inadvertent invitation to the nagging, judgmental voices that are ready to pop into your head. As long as you must work within the limitation of keeping your eyes bound to the subject, you have some protection from those old voices. If you find yourself plagued by voices, I recommend several possible remedies:

- Ask the voice to go away, or just command it away.
- If it was helpful in the first place, continue to work within the limitation.
- Begin an ongoing dialogue with your pencil. Talk about every move and curve of the line you are traveling. This dialogue will drown out the critical voice, at least while you're drawing.

- If the voice persists (during work or after your drawing is finished), getting in the way of your drawing process, spend time dialoguing with it. Find out whose voice it is, if it will ever be satisfied, and what it wants from you.
- Combine this dialogue with some ritualizing to send this voice away or to turn it into a more benevolent and helpful partner.

➢After doing three seven-minute drawings of the exterior of this object (different views) spend some time contemplating what you have learned. Answer the following questions:

- How does this object face the world?
- What kind of surface does it have (i.e., rough, sensuous, brittle, etc.)?
- What new things did I learn about it (beyond the label)?
- Are there any similarities between this object and me?
- What kind of an exterior do I put out to the world? Smooth or rough?
- What labels do people use to describe me?
- What do others presume about me?
- After answering these questions, take a break. Give yourself some time to be with the lesson(s) you've just learned. If you didn't get much from the exercise, don't worry about it; just stay with the sensory experience of the drawing process itself.

If you're trying to evaluate your progress, remember that there are many different ways of developing skills. Of course, you want to feel that your drawing skill is progressing. If your ability to see is improving, your ability to draw is improving. Even if this is not yet showing up in the images on paper, please trust the power of your eyes, and stay with it. Do as many exterior drawings as you like before moving on.

Personal growth is another important element to drawing meditation. The questions regarding your exterior as reflected by the chosen object can give you important insights about yourself. Even if your drawing isn't what you'd like it to be, if your new sight has grown from the subject to yourself, then you've made a different type of progress.

The third type of progress is in the depth of connection you're learning to make with "inanimate" objects. This connectedness has the power to resonate throughout your life. If all the world's citizens practiced this seeing meditation, we'd all eventually realize that the poisons that pollute the Earth's rivers contaminate our own bloodstreams, and that the toxic waste dumped into the Earth's body clogs our own pores. If you are learning to make these kinds of connections, you are making progress, and your drawings will reflect the compassion you bring to all things.

➤When you return to your work space, clear away all thoughts of the exterior. Its time to go inside the subject, and again I suggest that you take a moment to ask permission. When you open your eyes, let the object know that you will enter with great reverence. This is especially important if you will be cutting into the object (tomatoes, apples, peaches, etc.).

➤After you have revealed the interior of your subject and set your timer for a ten-minute drawing, take a moment to relax into the rhythm of your breath. Be sure to have extra paper nearby, though I suggest that you again put the next two drawings on one sheet.

➤Do two ten-minute drawings of the interior of this object, taking a five- to ten-minute break between drawings. Then direct the above reflection questions toward the interior of the object. On a separate sheet of paper (perhaps in your journal), set up a list of comparative qualities.

Example

Object	Myself
Must be cut into to get to the interior	Hard to let people into my private self; they must really dig to get me to reveal myself.
Once the interior is revealed, nothing is hidden	Once I let someone in, I feel very open and visible, vulnerable, in fact. Do others feel the same when they let me in?

You can summarize your exterior/interior study as you wish. You may want to ritualize the entire experience. If you do this exercise with a group, I would suggest that you spend some time in pairs discussing the experience. Encourage dialogue and shared observations from partners; these observations can bring about important breakthroughs into personal insight.

Toward Love and Wisdom

The message came after long patient waiting with an openness to hear. But it came in another way, it was my interaction with the stone as I drew her that made the message clear. As she showed her facets and lines I was curiously attracted to the different perspectives the stone could be seen from. As I played with perspective the details of each face changed from a bold, up front, intuitive line to hiding where I could not draw him out. I was seduced in this play to draw and draw and draw. As my drawings continued they became more abstract, the details faded and the shape was all that was present. Again, I learned that it is the perspective I take, how present I am that determines what details I look at and how each facet of the whole expresses to me.

MARILYN GUY

This work has an added dimension when it is applied to personal relationships. Earlier in this chapter we talked about labels in regard to objects, but it's also easy for us to get caught up in the labels we use for people. (Perhaps the exterior/interior exercise taught you about labels others may use for you.) We can fall asleep in the comfort zone of labels, and no longer see anyone's personhood. When I define my mother only according to a label, I lose sight of the person she is. This is a form of sedation, a form of sleepwalking from which too many people suffer. It makes us unavailable to loved ones, friends, and colleagues. Looking at a significant person through a drawing meditation may help you to see that person honestly for the first time.

Drawing meditation requires soul engagement, which is at the core of all good communication as well as good art. I would love to see family members do drawing meditations with each other. After every person had drawn everyone else they could do a facilitated follow-up discussion about what new things they'd learned. I am convinced that this type of time spent together would greatly diminish tension and improve communication. (Family members might even find they can have fun together.)

As you become more proficient at this drawing meditation process, your work will begin to take on integrity. A certain quality of honesty will emerge. If, after a considerable dedication to this process, you are not able to see some recognizable presence of the subject in your drawing (I hate to tell you this, but . . .), you're probably not seeing it. Don't fool yourself: that is always the case. Please don't chide yourself; you just need to slow down both your internal process and the drawing process. Ask yourself if the desire for a finished product isn't getting in your way.

When you're feeling that you have begun to develop a level of proficiency and are enjoying the drawing process, study the drawings of the great masters (the library is filled with great books). This, of course, is for the sake of learning, not comparison. Many of Picasso's drawings have more honesty, courage, and power than his paintings. Dürer, Matisse, Kollwitz, Schiele: the works of these artists, along with your own ongoing experience, will train you toward a growing knowledge of and satisfaction with drawing.

Exercise: Drawing Meditation
Session 3—The Counsel of Stone

The Counsel of Stone is to be done in several stages. The final segment is not drawn but painted. Allow at least three hours. Consult resource 1 for questions concerning the proper use and care of materials before doing part 3. Lastly, be sure to read through the full description of the project before you begin so you'll know where you're going. (Please do not facilitate a group in this meditation before you have done it yourself.)

This meditation is designed from a common practice among Native Americans: the tradition of seeking counsel from animals and stones. The more comfortable you are with the drawing process, the more you will be able to concentrate on your communion with the stone. When you feel that you can look down occasionally without breaking your rhythm or concentration, you're ready to do this project.

If your internal judge is still lecturing you, try a few more practice sessions, and perform a ritual that invokes the voice of a mentor or supporter to tell the judge to leave.

Once again we can turn to the vision and the song of the poet to lead us into this experience. The poet Charles Simic must surely have spent as much time with his stone as Rilke spent with the panther in order to give us the following poem, entitled simply, "Stone."

> Go inside a stone.
> That would be my way.
> Let somebody else become a dove
> Or gnash with a tiger's tooth.
> I am happy to be a stone.
>
> From the outside the stone is a riddle:
> No one knows how to answer it.
> Yet within, it must be cool and quiet
> Even though a child throws it in a river;
> The stone sinks, slow, unperturbed
> To the river bottom
> Where the fishes come to knock on it
> And listen.

I have seen sparks fly out
When two stones are rubbed,
So perhaps it is not dark inside after all;
Perhaps there is a moon shining
From somewhere, as though behind a hill—
Just enough light to make out
The strange writings, the star-charts
On the inner walls.*

Supplies

* Newsprint paper
* White drawing paper
* A 2B graphite pencil
* India ink
* A rock (not smooth)
* A #6 pointed brush
* An audible timer
* A half-inch flat-edge brush
* A fine-point felt-tip pen
* A three-inch flat-edge wash brush
* Containers for water and ink

Getting to Work

Finding the stone who will counsel you may be a separate project. It might even be done on a different day. You may want to take a walk, or meditate in your own garden. The search for the stone may be part of a ritual. You may have a rock that has been with you for a long time that you would like to connect with in this way. Because of the linear nature of this type of contour drawing, I ask people not to work with a very smooth stone, which gives only a singular and regular external line.

---

* Quoted in Bly, *News of the Universe*, 248.

Part I

➤When you have found your rock and are ready to begin drawing, you may want to burn some incense and/or play some Native American flute music. Take time for breathing and centering to take you into a dark, calm place at the core of your body. Close your eyes and feel the natural rhythm of your breathing. Slowly let go of all your other concerns. Allow your breath to expand, releasing the tension in your neck, shoulders, and back.

➤With only the rock, pencil, paper, and timer in front of you, place your focus on the rock. As in the basic Drawing Meditation exercise, begin this meditation not by drawing, but rather by looking. Leave the pencil on the table. Set the timer for two minutes. Allow your eye to travel over the surface of the subject ever so slowly, creeping along the visible lines. Continue to do this (with or without music) for the full two minutes.

➤At the end of the two minutes, close your eyes. See the rock in your mind's eye. Try to follow those lines, just as you did with your eyes open. Do not be discouraged if you can't see the lines clearly; remember that the point is to connect with the stone in a way that transcends your usual physical presence. This form of seeing develops a depth of vision that recognizes our mutual atomic and spiritual existence. After all, the basic difference between you and the rock is only the structure of your molecules.

➤When you feel that you have come to the end of this stage of the meditation (this should take no less than a full minute) open your eyes once again, allowing them to stop at one spot on the rock surface. Reestablish your optical connection with the subject, and when you feel accepted into its space, pick up your pencil and begin to record the journey your eye makes along the rock body. I suggest that you do at least three seven-minute drawings, turning the rock after each one.

➤When you're finished, spend a little time reflecting on the drawings and the rock. Then set them aside, and take up a sheet of the white drawing paper and your felt-tip pen (if you don't have a felt pen use a soft lead pencil). During the next drawing give yourself permission to "check in" frequently with the image you're creating on the paper.

Keep in mind that this drawing should be large enough to create a composition on the whole page. You may want to combine several views of the stone into one composition. This drawing will be about the essence of your "companion," its "rockness." For the moment, stay focused on its lines only.

By this time you're becoming fairly familiar with its rock body, so when you're content with the linear study you've created, begin to look at other qualities on the surface. Add any interesting marks or patterns you've discovered.

Part II

The next segment of this project introduces you to the use of India ink. If time is a problem, and you'd like to do this segment on a separate day, stop here. If you're already well familiarized with India ink or watercolors, you may decide to go on to part 3.

➤To begin, lay out the rest of the materials listed above, plus a clean piece of white drawing paper for experimentation. Whenever you're painting, you should have rags or paper towels handy. Obviously, working near a sink is helpful.

➤Set your rock and drawing aside.

➤Have ready a large container of water and a number of smaller ones for mixing the ink with varying amounts of water. India ink is extremely dense, and a beautiful array of gray shades can be easily achieved by mixing ink with varying amounts of water.

➤Take a little time to experiment with this graying process. Use a practice piece of paper. Put a little ink into one of the small containers. Add a small amount of water. Wet your half-inch flat-edge brush, and squeeze out excess water with your fingers (always moving out away from the brush well—the metal under which bristles are attached to the handle). Dip the brush into the watered-down ink, make a graceful stroke on the page, and watch the ink glide onto the white page.

➤Quickly dip your brush back into the water, then back to the stroke on the page. Overlap this brush stroke by about a quarter of an inch, and follow it as exactly as possible. Watch the water draw the ink, creating a feathered edge and yet another shade of gray.

Rock Painting by Paul Belhumeur

➤Following this kind of playful experimental format, spend approximately fifteen minutes getting acquainted with the medium. Don't expect to become an expert or to develop a lot of control in those fifteen minutes; this is only an introduction. I encourage you to play more with the India ink in your journal.

➤If you are scientifically minded, you can use the journal for a little research project. As you mix ink and water, measure the amounts with teaspoons or droppers. Record your gray shades in strips, circles, or squares, with the proportions for each shade written in pencil immediately below the sample.

➤When you have become better acquainted with the ink, I suggest you take a little break before going back to your rock drawing. Just a few minutes will do. Give yourself a sense of shifting gears. You will be returning now to the realm of the rock and will want to feel calm and centered.

Part III

➤Bring your rock and the large drawing back onto your work space. Hold the rock in your hands as you sit comfortably in your chair. Close your eyes and sink slowly into the calm darkness of your inner self. Feel the natural rhythm of your breathing. Slowly guide your focus from your head down through your neck. Watch for tension in your jaw; if you feel it, let it go, and do the same for your shoulders, spine, trunk, and legs. Feel your feet on the floor, and establish a sense of balance in your body.

➤Finally, place your focus on the stone in your hands. You have spent a good deal of time with this stone. You have trekked across its terrain, and you have drawn its lines over and over. In this part you will be expanding your portrait of the rock, but not before you allow it to become more intimate with you.

➤Feel the weight of the rock in your hands. This is the presence of the earth. With your eyes closed, let your fingers feel the lines that your eyes have traveled on. Allow its presence to fill you. It is a piece of your home. This stone is part of the ancient planet that sustains and nurtures you. This rock has earth wisdom, and it's time for you to listen to the Counsel of Stone.

➤I suggest a ritual gesture at this point. You might simply light a candle, or burn sage or incense. This might be a fitting time to reread Charles Simic's poem. Do whatever feels correct for you.

➤When you feel that you and this stone are in the proper positions and relationship to each other, ask what message the stone has brought you today. Hold it in your hands, reading the surface in a new way, seeing and hearing with open eyes, ears, and heart. I often find that some marking on the stone's surface leads me to the message. Be patient. If after ten to fifteen minutes you do not feel that you have received a message or lesson, ask yourself why you might not be ready to receive a gift from a stone.

➤When you have received the message (or perhaps the stone has challenged you with a question), set the stone in front of you with your large drawing. Place it in the position(s) it was in when you did the original drawing(s). Study what the light does to it. Do you see changes in colors? What kind of shapes and shadows do you see?

➤As you begin to translate the language of the eye to the language of the brush, please remember that the purpose of your painting is not to create a likeness of this rock.

Shall I say this again? The purpose of your painting is not to create a likeness of this rock.

I am emphatic about that, because I know that a certain percentage of people will now look at the rock and have a crisis of self-confidence. Please, relax. Go into the world of stone.

This rock has no expectations of you. It simply continues to reveal itself to you through the very nature of its being. I invite you to open yourself in a gesture of cosmic hospitality and gratitude. The inherent atomic activity going on within the rock, coupled with your own atomic energy, will create an image in black, gray, and white. All you have to do is let it happen.

➤If you want to use the wide wash brush, be sure to have a bowl or container wide enough so that the bristles will not be distorted. Keep your brushes wet; wet them before dipping them into the ink. As you paint on top of the drawing, allow new forms to be born. If you use a felt-tip pen, your initial lines will run. Just let them run. Keep working from the ink to the page to the stone, gathering nonrational information. Keep moving, and have fun. You can use your pencils with this painting, too.

Reflect on the message you just received, and begin to work it into the composition of this painting. I like to see the messages written on the paintings. You can decide whether you want it written on the bottom, across the image, or written on another sheet and attached somehow. Work with the washes and the India ink, pens, and pencils until you feel finished.

It's important to decide what you will do with the rock when you're finished. In some parts of the world, rocks are greatly revered and not to be removed from their natural place. In other places, you can feel free to adopt a rock. Many people like to keep special rocks on their altars. A friend of mine who leads vision quests and river trips in the Grand Tetons is never without at least one rock companion in his pocket. When I met him he was living in California, and those rocks (plus daily walks among the redwoods) kept him balanced and in touch with the earth.

Under the Rainbow

The chief aim of color should be to serve expression as well as possible.

HENRI MATISSE

The drawing process we have now begun expands our depth of vision beyond the limitations of conventional, undeveloped sight into seeing on a grander scale. Our body is more receptive than we realize. It actually sees through the entire sensory system. The objects we see enter us through our optic nerve, our olfactory system, and our sense of touch. When we become conscious of seeing, we dare to open ourselves to the world around us. We become aware of our porosity, allowing images to enter and move through us. With this kind of sight comes an experience of intimacy with the world that may be a little frightening at first. It's important to remember that we are adaptable creatures, and that our organism adjusts to this new sight. As we begin to see sharper images, as things seem closer to us, our intuitive powers grow. We develop an ability to grasp and understand the unseen or nonrational elements around us. Learning to see with the eyes of the soul allows us to caress the world through sight.

Can you remember the first time you saw a rainbow? Can you remember the magical quality rainbows had for you when you were a child? Reflecting on that experience may bring you to an understanding of what is meant by seeing with the eyes of the soul. Children embrace the world with their eyes: bears in zoos, ponies in movies, and rainbows in the sky. We are creatures who naturally love the world.

As we grow into adults, we may become too emotionally hardened and intellectually sophisticated to experience the world through our soul. We work from our brain so we can "stay on top of things." But certain things in this world don't allow us to suppress their spiritual exuberance—for example, colors. Our response to color is totally nonintellectual and nonrational. Of course, as painters we need to have some type of understanding about color, so at this point I'll introduce you to the *color wheel.*

Being an artist means: not numbering and counting, but ripening like a tree, which doesn't force its sap, and stands confidently in the storms of spring, not afraid that afterward summer may not come. It does come. But it comes only to those who are patient, who are there as if eternity lay before them, so unconcernedly silent and vast. I learn it every day of my life, learn it with pain I am grateful for: patience is everything.

RAINER MARIA RILKE

Viriditas

The work of the great Rhineland visionary, Hildegard of Bingen, supplies the basic theme of this color experience. Hildegard, whose works have been recently rediscovered and celebrated, was a "Renaissance woman" long before that epoch. Born in 1098, she became one of the most influential women of her time. Aside from her work as a Benedictine abbess, Hildegard was a leading intellectual, healer, composer, writer, and painter.

She coined the term *viriditas* to express nature's power to birth and nurture life. Growing up in the lush verdancy of Rhineland Germany,

Hildegard saw a divine presence in her surroundings. From that verdancy her writings became filled with metaphor: "the verdancy of justice," "the greening power of faith," "the vigor that hugs the world." Hildegard's spirituality was a tapestry of faith, compassion, and love of the earth. She measured the health and well-being of people and situations according to their harmony with nature.

HOMAGE TO HILDEGARD 1980

> The air,
> with its penetrating strength,
> characterizes
> the victorious banner that is trust.
>
> It gives light
> to the fire's flame
> and sprinkles
> the imagination of believers
> with the dew of hope.
>
> Thus does trust show the way.
> Those who breathe this dew
> long for heavenly things.
> They carry within
> refreshing,
> fulfilling,
> greening love,
> with which they hasten to the aid of all.
>
> With the passion of heavenly yearning,
> they produce rich fruit.*

The contemporary poet Dylan Thomas expressed a similar relationship to the power of natural forces in the opening stanzas of his poem "The Force That Through the Green Fuse Drives the Flower." This, too, is a poem about greening power.

> The force that through the green fuse drives the flower
> Drives my green age; that blasts the roots of trees
> Is my destroyer.
> And I am dumb to tell the crooked rose
> My youth is bent by the same wintry fever.

---

* Gabriele Uhlein, *Meditations with Hildegard of Bingen* (Santa Fe, NM: Bear & Co., 1982), 69.

The force that drives the water through the rocks
Drives my red blood; that dries the mouthing streams
Turns mine to wax.
And I am dumb to mouth unto my veins
How at the mountain spring the same mouth sucks.*

* *The Poems of Dylan Thomas* (New York: New Directions, 1971), 77.

Exercise: *Viriditas*

The exercise on the following pages can play an important part in your developing a certain self-confidence when handling colors. The aim of the project is to awaken your eye to color, as it has been awakened to line and form through the drawing meditation. Remember that this is only a beginning; I suggest that you begin to look at the works of other painters to study how color can be used to make an impact.

Part I

Spend some time familiarizing yourself with the color wheel.

The three *primary colors* are those that cannot be mixed; we get them from the earth. The primaries are yellow, red, and blue. *Secondary colors* are those that can be made by mixing the primary colors. Secondary colors are orange (a mixture of red and yellow), green (a mixture of blue and yellow), and violet or purple (a mixture of red and blue).

You will notice that black and white do not exist on the color wheel. They are not colors; rather they are the lack of all color (black) or the presence of all color (white). Adding black to a color gives you shading; that is, you will have the same color, but it will be a bit darker than when you started. Adding white at increasing intervals will give you a range of tints, lighter shades of the same color.

Supplies

* Tempera paints in primary colors—yellow, red, and blue—plus black, white, and green
* Multipurpose vellum paper, two sheets

*   A #6 brush (flat-edge or pointed)
*   A #2 pencil
*   Water, containers, palette, kneaded eraser, paper towels

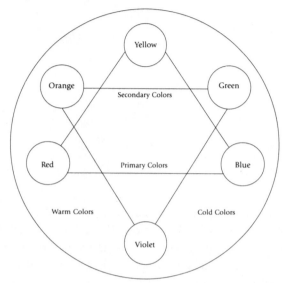

The Color Wheel

*The Color Wheel: Infinite Mandala**

I like to think of the color wheel as the infinite mandala, because it is an infinitely expandable circle. Between the primary and secondary colors there are *tertiary colors* such as yellow-orange, blue-violet, chartreuse (yellow-green), and so on. You can see that as these colors are inserted into the scheme of the wheel, the mandala expands with limitless possibilities.

Getting to Work

For this exercise you may begin in one of two ways: you may place a shade of purchased green (predetermined by the manufacturer) on your palette, or you may begin with blue and yellow to mix your own beginning green. When you have a solid green color, place it in the center of the

---

* See "The Mandala—A Painting of Balance and Wholeness on pg. 134.

palette. Place a small amount of black and white (with space between them) on the outer perimeters of the palette, or, better still, on a separate palette. You will be focusing on creating greens by mixing the green on the palette with each primary color, beginning with red, so to begin, place some red on the palette.

You may want to play with the brush a bit on a piece of scratch paper to develop a consistent brush stroke. The practice sheet looks like a meditation when it's finished if all the brush strokes are alike and placed in some sort of pattern.

➤Place a good-sized sheet of paper on your work space.

➤Dip the brush into the water; pull a small amount of green out of the center halfway toward the red. Quickly rinse any green off the brush and pull some of the red to the green. Mix these with a gentle stirring motion of the brush (try not to get a lot of paint up into the brush).

➤If the paint is too thick to stir easily, add water. When the two colors have become one, make one of your predetermined strokes on the page. The paint should not be so thick that it stands up off the page, nor should it be so watery that it won't hold the form of your stroke.

➤Set down your brush. Under the stroke, write in pencil the proportions and colors that created the color. For example: "1/1, red/green." For each of the next strokes you can add increasing amounts of red, which can be notated either individually with the measurement of the increment or simply with a phrase such as "incremental additions of red to green." If your colors are named, then the name should definitely be included, as you would get different results working with, say, cobalt blue than you would from ultramarine blue.

➤You can experiment with the additions of black or white to a particular color; just remember to record the components below any color that goes on your color chart. Continue with red until you feel ready to go on. You do not necessarily have to remove the red from the palette. You may decide to add it as a third dimension to future combinations.

➤Next, add yellow to your palette, and proceed as you did for red. As the chart develops you will gain an inner connection to these colors on the page. These are not random hues; they are the colors you have created yourself. Some of them may not even look like green, but you are now learning the invisible elements of color that will empower your paintings in the future. *Viriditas,* greening power, is not always green!

➤Remember the importance of rinsing the brush out frequently as you go along. This will ensure the clear mixing of colors. Dragging the old colors into the new ones will "contaminate" the freshness of new combinations. Eventually, colors could become muddy.

➤When you have finished mixing the range of blue and green combinations, set your chart somewhere to dry. The second part of this exercise can be done immediately or on the next day. Don't let too much time elapse; it's important to do part 2 while your memory of achieving these colors is fresh.

Part II

Part 2 is a nice break from your studio space. Take a walk outside. Collect examples of green from nature (a dozen if possible), and take them back to the painting area with you.

Lay nature's greens next to your greens. Which ones have you already created, and what colors combined to create them? Use the nature greens that you have not already created as a challenge. Mix your pigments to match them.

When you're finished with this exercise, you can staple, glue, or sew your living greens onto your "greening power" page and hang it in your work studio for future reference. You can create a chart like this for each color if you like. The charts create a colorful and useful atmosphere. I keep a small spiral notebook with color swatches, which are often helpful when I'm struggling with a painting's color problems.

I think you now understand what I mean when I say that a reverential eye caresses the world. The eye itself is not judgmental; it is receptive and hospitable. For a painter, sight is the link between the sacred and the social self. The pursuit of personal imagery and self-knowledge leads us eventually deeper into community with all creatures and ultimately with the cosmos.

With a reverential eye, let's move into the ring of culture and society.

CHAPTER FOUR

Expanding
into the Social Self

as you may have gathered, our course of development has been slowly moving out from the core of divinity in the center of our original diagram. We are now at the threshold of the social self. The issues and questions of human social adaptation have spawned some of the great creative efforts of humankind. Myths, plays, poetry, and schools of psychological theory are available to us as tools of understanding and celebration.

This formulation of the social self has evolved through my experience as artist and teacher in order to deal with certain essential issues that determine the creative realizations of the individual. The following are the issues I have thus far found most essential in personal creative development:

- Autonomy
- Play
- Solitude versus loneliness
- Self-love and well-being
- Social security and trust
- Healing
- Integrity

In chapters 4 and 5 we will look at these issues as we move outward toward the realm of the universal self. The exercises will expand to projects with other people. You might want to think about the people you would most like to work with and give them some time to read the earlier segments, or talk to them about what you've been doing so far.

Play and Autonomy

We have talked a great deal already about play, and in chapter 1 we discussed the evolution from autonomous play to competitive game play. If you think back over your early years, you will probably remember an overlapping time when you enjoyed meaningless play with friends as well as game play. Some of our fondest childhood memories are those of silly games and antics carried on with playmates. Rolling on grass, hanging upside down, spinning until we fell down—all these activities were really based on fun.

As adults we don't often have opportunities to interact in a group on a spontaneous, imaginative level. Usually, group situations tend to make us self-conscious and defensive. Whether with relatives, acquaintances, or strangers, we often don't feel safe to take the kinds of risks that creativity and spontaneity require. As most of us are constantly called on to work cooperatively in family and business situations, it's important to find a way to remain relaxed, self-confident, and creative in these circumstances.

Learn to Take Your Fun Seriously

In Creative Meditation we are constantly rejuvenated by returning spiritually and psychologically to memories of childhood playfulness as the genesis of adult creativity. In childhood we didn't need to be taught to follow our fun. Taking fun seriously is an important lesson to be resurrected from our memory banks.

By opening ourselves to the social aspects of our creativity, we can create new experiences of play and enjoyment that revitalize our childhood talent for it. Our early excitement came from the anticipation of experience rather than expectations of success. Part of the joy of going down the slide, splashing in water, or swinging came from anticipation of the experience. We still experience this in adulthood, but it is often entangled with expectations of personal performance. A precious gift of childhood, which we lose all too soon, is the freedom from the need to succeed at everything. We can become so failure-phobic that we're paralyzed, unable to try anything new for fear of looking foolish or failing to do it immediately like a virtuoso. Painting and drawing with no product orientation can give you the pleasure of simple delight. The joy is in the experience. Even for professional artists, the seduction of painting is the ecstasy of the creative moment. Those moments are available to everyone.

Sharing the painting and drawing experience with others adds to the playful dimension when you delight in the activity; sharing the goo of the paint and the charge of the colors, the spiritual light that begins to glow throughout the group. Think of becoming light-hearted, of having a heart that is lit with the creative energy of the human spirit. This is the essence of the cocreative painting experience.

Take a moment to savor another childhood memory. Go back to a memory of laughter, an occasion of play with friends. You might have been doing cartwheels at the beach, playing tag, or rolling around on a newly cut lawn. Go deeply into this memory, remembering the way the laughter felt in your body. Try to remember the smells in the air and the breeze or the stillness. Bring back the sound of the laughter of your friends around you.

Write your reflections on that memory, and answer the following questions.

➤What kind of game or activity were you engaged in?

➤How did it start and end?

➤What do you remember of the interaction between playmates?

➤Was there something in that experience that you no longer have in your life? (Frivolity? Folly? Camaraderie?)

➤Do you want to reclaim this missing ingredient?

➤How could you bring it into your life?

To understand the creative dimensions of the social self, we need to consider the socialization process that the personal self goes through. Unfortunately, not all our memories of this socialization process are as sweet as the memory of fun with our pals. Most of us have plenty of mental memorabilia of the deliberate and nondeliberate lessons that taught us to be acceptable members of society. (Some of us are still trying to decide how much of this we want to go along with!) Whether we got them from parents or teachers, we all remember edicts such as "sit up straight," "don't talk with your mouth full," and "don't pick your nose." These became boring litanies to our children's ears, though as adults we've come to realize that a certain amount of direction was necessary. Directing the budding personal self into a social self is a delicate and critical task, and the style of that direction makes the difference between a fondly remembered childhood and a painful one.

It is only natural that the early sense of autonomy, which was unselfconscious, is overridden by authority figures and peer group pressure. The ego develops as an expression of the personal self and responds to the environment in such a way as to maintain health and an inner balance.

The emotional handicaps we carry concerning our creativity and self-esteem are the result of wounds received during the early socialization period. The most crippling blow is the betrayal of the trust inherent in young children. The social self is the cultural adaptation of the vulnerable personal self, and our early experiences are the catalysts for the development of self-protective mechanisms. The wounds inflicted (perhaps unwittingly) by those we most trusted and loved are the hardest to heal, because they become an integral part of our self-identity.

The autonomy regained through the Creative Meditation process is grounded in a reverence for our selfhood, a reclaiming of authority, a willingness to follow spontaneous urges, and a sense of cosmic permission. Working in groups, we recognize our mutual struggles and give respectful space and support. This group attitude ensures everyone's emotional safety and relaxation.

Solitude and Loneliness

In *Beyond Psychology*, psychologist Otto Rank, whose work deals largely with the psyche of the artist, focuses his attention on an important pivotal issue in individual development. "Man's eternal conflict," says Rank, "is the struggle between his need for likeness and his desire for difference."* This conflict may have come to us for the first time when we traded free autonomous play for group play, or when a new child was born into our family. Whatever the case, throughout our lives we work to establish a balance between recognition for singular achievement and the camaraderie of group acceptance.

Rank and contemporary Swiss psychologist Alice Miller each recognize that this paradox of social adaptability has an important anthropological component: group consciousness carried as a psychological factor from our ancestral primal experience. We have a genetic drive toward community, and an intellectual drive toward autonomy and distinction.

We are forced to confront this paradoxical situation anew throughout our lives. The decisions we make, even as children, shape our lives, our self-image, and our self-esteem, and the inherent factor within *every* decision is an awareness of solitude. The outcome of each choice eventually determines whether that solitude is friend or foe.

Creativity is a spiritual action in which a person forgets about himself, moves outside of himself in the creative act, absorbed by his task.

NICHOLAS BERDYAEV

---

* Otto Rank, *Beyond Psychology* (New York: Dover Publications, 1941), 99.

Exercise:
Reflection #3

Man's eternal conflict is the struggle between his need for likeness and his desire for difference.

—OTTO RANK

Spend some time reflecting on the quotation above and how it pertains to your life. Then answer the questions below. These questions could also provide an excellent springboard for family or group discussion.

➤How has this conflict played a role in your life?

➤How has it affected your creative development?

➤To what degree does it continue to affect your creative development?

➤Do you want to change this? What is your first possible step?

Do something that requires you to take a creative risk. Below, describe this creative risk and its outcome.

Self-Love and Well-Being— Toward a Healthy Social Self

In *The Drama of the Gifted Child,* Alice Miller talks about depression and the issue of adaptability in our contemporary individualistic society.

> Depression is a disease of our time. Within a culture that was shielded from other value systems, such as that of orthodox Jewry in the ghetto, or of Negro families in the Southern states a hundred years ago, an adapted individual was not autonomous and did not have his own individual sense of identity (in our sense) that could have given him support; but he did feel supported by the group. . . . Today it is hardly possible for any group to remain so isolated from others who have different values. Therefore it is necessary today for the individual to find his support within himself, if he is not to become the victim of various interests and ideologies. This strength within himself through access to his own real needs and feelings and the possibility of expressing them—thus becomes crucially important for him on the one hand, and on the other is made enormously more difficult through living in contact with various different value systems. These factors can probably explain the rapid increase of depression in our time and also the general fascination with various groups.*

The "various groups" to which Miller refers are those that offer a base of support and an escape from the solitude that has turned to loneliness. Since people have moved away from small, sometimes tribal or tribelike communities, Miller points out, individuals lack a sense of group identification, belonging, understanding, and acceptance. A person who feels socially stable can enjoy alone time as a creative luxury, but social instability leaves the individual hungry for self-esteem and confidence. The personal self and the social self are inextricably linked. Without affiliation we can feel lost and adrift in the sea of humanity. Our natural longing for community draws us together in church groups, fraternal organizations, clubs, even cults. These are our cultural lifeboats.

Yet the depression to which Miller refers is a product of alienation, an alienation that can build up even within the environment of a community. The essential ingredients for inner peace and a healthy life are self-love and self-acceptance.

---

* Alice Miller, *The Drama of the Gifted Child* (New York: Basic Books, 1981), 59.

Here again, an understanding of inherent affirmation provides the support that lies beyond the immediate circumstance. We can simultaneously honor our natural drives toward community and autonomy, and still free ourselves from the sense of competition that grows out of self-doubt. While competition can be constructive in challenging each of us to our finest efforts, an understanding of inherent affirmation allows for competitiveness that is not personally destructive.

Social Security and Trust

Through the energy of inherent affirmation, the ancestral self can be the creative resource for both the vulnerable personal self and the adaptable social self. Evidence is abundant in proving that the connection with ancestral and cultural traditions can confirm creative expression and bring communities together. Murals painted on public buildings in a Hispanic neighborhood, for example, carry on a common cultural tradition and are recognized as the expression of an entire community. The same is true of gospel music in African-American neighborhoods, or strains of regionally evolved country music such as bluegrass, Zydeco, or Tex-Mex. Communal pride and joy are the outcome of collective creativity.

The creative process catches us at the junction of our conflicting urges. The act of expression can give us a sense of alienation, of being "other," but when we share the process of creativity the sense of alienation is conquered. The bridging between these paradoxical impulses is the ability to remain focused on a deeply personal process, knowing that when the work is done we will have related to society in a meaningful way.

I encourage students to share their work with each other, because it also teaches them not to take themselves too seriously. The Creative Meditation environment must be a nurturing one where the creative evolution of each person can unfold. Though creative work comes from a genuine and spiritual effort, we need to keep a healthy perspective about what we're doing. In a compassionate environment every participant can trust in the support of the group and can trust the input of others for evaluation and new ideas.

Realizing that we live in a global village challenges us to pool our creative energies for the development of an optimistic future. The shared Creative Meditation experience can establish the type of communal trust needed to make the world community the primary support for the creativity of all people.

It is the passion of the artist . . . to communicate what he experiences as the subconscious and unconscious significance of his relation to his world. "Communicate" is related to "commune," and, in turn, both are avenues to the experience of communion and community with our fellow space men.

ROLLO MAY

This trust must exist on five levels:

1. Trust in the facilitator/teacher
2. Trust in one's self
3. Trust in the medium
4. Trust in the process
5. Trust in a divine creative force

Trust in the Facilitator/Teacher

If you have been following the activities and considering the ideas in this book, you are trusting in me as your current facilitator. It's impossible for us to have the type of relationship we'd have in a studio classroom setting, but your continuing receptivity to these pages is an expression of trust.

Trust in One's Self

In the long run it will matter less to you that I trust in your inherent creative ability than that *you* have come to trust in yourself. Trust your intentions and the power of your desire. Everything you create comes from your desire and your courage to follow through.

Self-trust is a persistent issue for everyone and is probably the most important item on this list. My definition of maturity is ongoing personal growth through flexibility, curiosity, and a constantly increasing capacity for self-trust.

The experiences of childhood—learning to work on goals others had decided upon, developing work habits that were not natural to our own process and rhythm, and being evaluated according to the expectations and desires of authority figures—did not prepare us for a self-trusting, healthy adulthood. Even well-meaning educators were striving more for manageable obedience than the chaos of a flowering natural curiosity and creative impulse that would have led to exploration and experimentation. The result of all this was a spiritual and behavioral domination that has seeped into our psyches and continues to suppress creativity.

We must claim a healthy and creative adulthood for ourselves. We can choose not to reaffirm the unfortunate lessons of earlier years; we can choose to change. We can be self-supportive, and we can support each other. We can give ourselves a pat on the back from time to time and share our work with trusted friends. We can use meditation as a means of reconnecting with the inherent affirmation of our ancestors.

Find at least one other person with whom you can share your story. I suggest that you get together for dinner or lunch, to make this an enjoyable communion experience. If everyone agrees, you might want to record this conversation for future reflection.

Ask yourselves the following questions:

• What kind of attitudes contributed to our opinions of our creativity?

• What did we each learn from our environment about creativity in general, and about "creative or arty people"?

• How has this influenced the way we each approach the possibility of embracing our own creative self?

One evening I was having dinner with some friends and we got into a discussion about our childhoods. There were four of us at the table: a furniture designer and house painter, a figurative clay sculptor and mask maker, an architect and stone sculptor, and myself. We talked about our families' attitudes toward our creative leanings and aspirations. One person said that his family told him he wasn't smart enough to be a professional artist. A second person's family said she was too smart to be an artist. Another family felt that it would be a great embarrassment for their offspring to go into the arts as a profession, and yet another felt that such an aspiration was inconsistent with family history and the reality of racial limitations in the United States. Sharing our stories allowed us to laugh at ourselves and the contrasting idiosyncratic myths and presumptions of our families. We wondered if we had become artists because we were smarter or more stupid than the norm. We shared and understood the common battle scars that had grown out of our struggles toward a creative life. The ability to share our stories and struggles with each other was enormously healing for each of us.

In your painting journal spend time with these questions. Intermingle your thoughts with crayon and pencil doodles, colors, or images that express your feelings about these questions in nonverbal ways. Perhaps this nonverbal approach can be part of your conversation as well.

Realize that historical images of the artist also feed into our self-image. We Americans have a cartoon figure of the artist: this figure wears a beret and a smock, and carries a wooden palette. The artist in this image is always male. If you are a woman having trouble seeing yourself as a creative person, this sexist element of the stereotype may be contributing to your problem. Try this simple experiment: quickly name five well-known artists throughout history. How many women are on your list? Can you name five famous women artists? (That's Georgia O'Keeffe plus four others.)

I hope this little insight will help men and women realize that women have an even greater struggle seeing themselves as artists because the society fails to reveal, reflect, or affirm that image. This situation has forced women to reclaim their own history, and there is a great deal more data on women now available than ever before.

The important thing is to realize and name the factors that have been contributing to your self-doubts. By consciously ridding yourself of useless stereotypes, learned presumptions, and old myths, you will open new avenues of self-trust and new vistas of potential. In turn you will be removing lenses that have distorted your vision of yourself and the world. Creative Meditation is self-nurturing prayer. The more self-trust you exhibit, the more is generated.

Trust in the Medium

Many people are intimidated by paint and pencils because they feel they have no control over them, and it can be embarrassing to feel so challenged by inert objects. While I am always challenged by the prospect of my next artistic venture, I've never experienced intimidation, because crayons and paints were my childhood playmates. Growing up as an only child I spent many hours alone with my crayons, coloring books, and drawing papers. I saw my crayons as a community of personalities who were my friends. There were friendships between certain colors and disharmonies among others. I would actually dialogue with these colors as I used them, and they would tell me what had been going on while I was away. If a color sat in the box for too long, I felt its loneliness and would find a job for it.

I'm not suggesting that you think of crayons the way I did as a child, but we need to recognize that as modern people we have become extremely anthropocentric, and the only time we acknowledge a community is when we see a community of other humans. This memory is evidence of a child's ability to extend her emotional reality into an inanimate world. While we may see that childhood behavior as anthropocentric, it was not a way of cutting off from the world, but rather an attempt to commune with it. My crayons were my community. As a creative person you will come to realize that your media, the inanimate objects that are your tools, are also a part of your creative community.

Trusting the medium means learning about the materials with which you are working so that their limitations, their predictable and unpredictable qualities, become a part of your creative experience. Within this trust, you'll learn that paint, paper, and implements may create unintentional dimensions of your work. Eventually you'll come to look forward to the surprises rather than feeling a tense need to maintain control. The best way to develop this trust is to paint! Paint! Paint! The more experience you have, the more new things you try, the more your knowledge and trust will grow. Let the paint, paper, and brush be your teacher.

Trust in the Process

In his book *Finding One's Way with Clay*, which applies as much to painting as it does to pottery, ceramist and dancer Paulus Berensohn reminds us: "It is as much a discipline to learn to follow what happens as to plan what happens. It's even possible," he goes on, "that your very lack of control may bear fruit; by moving you from one vision to another."* We can think of this as the constantly dynamic balance of yin and yang, receptivity and activity. Allow your images to grow and change through your interaction with the elements.

Artist Peter Rogers recounts the following experience of learning to trust the medium as an actively creative entity in his book *A Painter's Quest.* Remembering a painting he had done in London in 1960, he writes:

> I had been painting on a large board which I had placed flat on the floor, since I was working wet. I was trying to paint an oriental saint, seated in the lotus position, deep in meditation. I had no trouble stating the figure, but soon ran into problems when I tried to relate him to the surrounding space; nothing seemed to work, and at the end of the day, having made a big mess, I mopped up as much of it as I could and went to bed. In the morning when I returned to the studio, I found the saint sitting on a seashore. Behind him was a storm-tossed sea, while above him the whole firmament swirled in orbit. During the night the puddles of paint I had failed to wipe up had done amazing things. Except for a few flicks here and there to indicate waves, I decided not to touch it; it was far more interesting than anything I could have done intentionally.†

Many people believe that "real artists" simply decide on their subject and create exactly what they have envisioned. Rogers's experience, however, is the more usual occurrence for professional artists. Art is created

---

* Paulus Berensohn, *Finding One's Way with Clay* (New York: Simon & Schuster, 1972), 82, 91.

† Peter Rogers, *A Painter's Quest* (Santa Fe, NM: Bear & Co., 1987), 71.

from the dynamic interaction of the person and the materials. Anyone who paints enough will inevitably come to trust that some surprise will show up and make the whole process exciting and unpredictable. Here's the final lesson of Rogers's story.

> So it was that there in my New Mexico studio twelve years later, I decided to stop relying so much on my head and to see what happened if I relied more on accident. I had a dozen small birch panels cut and primed and, laying them on the floor, I proceeded to throw paint on them.*

Rogers's experience confirms that often images appear that were not consciously intended. Sometimes they are too powerful, too honest, or too intimidating for their creator to confront. Creative Meditation is concerned with expanding the full human experience, so I urge you to trust the creative process and accept these images when they express themselves.

> *You must give birth to your images. They are the future waiting to be born. . . . Fear not the strangeness you feel. The future must enter you long before it happens. . . . Just wait for the birth . . . for the hour of new clarity.*
> —RAINER MARIA RILKE

As Rilke expresses it, the future is the embryo growing within each human. Put in these terms, your creativity is the amniotic fluid in which the future is nurtured and then brought forth. Trust your images, because they belong to the whole world; do not abort those imaginative offspring that are the origins of tomorrow. Treat them as you would a premature birth. Take care of them and nurse them in private spaces, in journals and dreams. Work with your images in the privacy of your sketchbook. You need not reveal yourself to others, but you do need to receive the portion of your inner self that is, like your dreams, revealing itself to you.

The most courageous image, of course, is self-image. Dare to see yourself as a creative, fruitful person. This daring is the first step toward realizing personal power. I am challenging you to stretch your self-image as far as you can, first in fantasy, then in reality. Have fun playing Walter Mitty: run little movies in your head, seeing yourself doing the most exciting things you can imagine. When you are finished with your movie, ask yourself how much of that character you actually could be. How much could you be comfortably, and how much could you dare to be?

---

* Ibid., 71.

Originality

Whenever people work in groups, the issue of originality seems to be of some concern. Actually one of the best things about creative group experiences is the cross-fertilization of images. I emphasize the importance of this nonverbal "imaginal" dialogue to clear people's minds of the old childhood ideas about "copying." This idea is one more remnant from old paradigm education, and it can be very inhibiting. Images are not top secret information, and treating them as if they were precious gems of personal cleverness will never produce anything of real value.

The ancient Chinese understood originality to mean that which is connected to the Great Harmony: an original thing is something in harmony with its origins. In its wisdom about the inherent creative nature of the universe, *The I Ching* (*The Chinese Book of Changes*) says: "The clouds pass and the rain does its work, and all individual beings flow into their forms."*

While fulfilling our personal potential may not be as simple as falling rain, when we learn to rely on our intuitive instincts we realize that our human development is also a naturally organic form of planetary evolution. While the universe is the context in which you live and grow, you, as a unique matrix of elements, are the origin of all your work. The more deeply you know yourself, the greater your potential will be for expressing your personal response to the world around and within you.

If you see an image or a painting that strikes your imagination, you will automatically begin to interpret it. If you paint this image, you will be passing it through what painter Wassily Kandinsky referred to as "the inner form." Even if you re-created the image as exactly as possible, the work would have been done through your hand, having passed through your eyes and psyche.

The ultimate creative journey is inward, a journey toward our own point of origin. Remaining true to that inward process of our work challenges us to a greater issue than originality; it takes us to the depths of authenticity. This authenticity gives honesty to all we do; it renders genuine all that passes through us. We play our part, making our little marks, knowing that we have made our contribution to the whole and that evolution rests on the carrying forward of an aesthetic baton. We each hand our gifts on to those with the courage to pick them up.

Surrender

We eventually learn that if we surrender to the creative principle of the universe, time no longer pushes against us. All ideas of conflict, competi-

---

* Richard Wilhelm and Cary F. Baynes, *The I Ching* (Princeton, NJ: Princeton Univ. Press, 1967), 4.

tion, and achievement disappear. We are like the glider plane that floats gracefully as a part of the air mass. Our creativity becomes our vehicle to the self and the divine.

Trust in a Divine Creative Force

Now God longs for nothing from you more than that you should emerge from yourself in accord with your being as a creature, and that you should admit God within yourself.

—MEISTER ECKHART

What would you think about God if you had not been brought up as a social creature in the twentieth century? It is impossible to know the answer to this question. After so many centuries of organized religions, our ideas about God cannot be purely our own. At best we select from existing concepts until we are at peace with a definition of the divine. Our experience of God, however, is always purely our own. The above quotation from the great German Dominican philosopher Meister Eckhart expresses the essence of the sacredness of self. The word "admit" in this translation is pivotal. Admit means recognizing what exists, as well as letting in. Both are essential to the practice of Creative Meditation.

Eckhart is saying that the origin of the human, and therefore our work, is divinity itself. By recognizing the divine core from which our lives flow out, we also admit to the sacred dimension of our personal acts of creation.

Think of the people you have come to trust in your life. How did you learn to trust them? You probably trust people who have revealed themselves to you, those who trust you. You know those people. The most difficult thing about trusting God is knowing God. Unfortunately, though many of us have been taught about God, we have not been encouraged to know God on our own terms. I see this best illustrated by an image of orphans whose only knowledge of their parents has come from photo albums and the accountings of others. This alienation from God is a deeply felt deprivation.

The following excerpt from *Meditations with Meister Eckhart* beautifully states the connection between trusting God and opening to our creativity.

> Why is it that some people do not bear fruit?
> It is because they are so busy clinging
> to their egotistical attachments
> and so afraid of letting go and letting be
> that they have no trust

either in God
or in themselves.
Love cannot distrust.
It can only await the good trustfully.
No person could ever trust God too much.
Nothing people ever do
is as appropriate as great trust in God.
With such trust,
God never fails to accomplish great things.*

Coming to know your own creativity will better acquaint you with the mysteries, surprises, and joyful potential of the universe. The more you open yourself to this unself-conscious process, the more you will recognize communion with others, human and nonhuman, animate and inanimate. To know the joy of painting is to open the doors of the soul.

---

* Matthew Fox, *Meditations with Meister Eckhart* (Santa Fe, NM: Bear & Co., 1982), 8.

Exercise: Partner Painting—
A Nonverbal Conversation

The following exercise introduces us to a new awareness of how we can create with others. To begin your creative outreach experience, select one person to work with. If this person has no background or understanding of the Creative Meditation approach, you will need to explain a bit about the work you have done thus far, and set their mind at ease about expectations and assumptions. Be sure they know that you have chosen them because of who they are and your relationship to them, not because you expect great artistic achievements from them. Be very specific about this; do not assume that they understand this point. Both partners should feel comfortable and at ease. The conversation you're about to have is meant to be fun.

Supplies

* 1 large sheet of paper
* Brushes—2 sets: one large two- or three-inch wash brush, one half-inch flat-edge brush, one pointed-tip #6 brush
* Tempera paints in your choice of assorted colors
* Watercolor pencils and/or crayons, regular crayons (optional)
* Water and clean-up paraphernalia
* Music: your choice of gentle, unobtrusive music. It should not become the topic of your conversation.

Preparation

The idea of this painting is to create a nonverbal dialogue with another person; in order to do this, a little personal preparation is required. The two of you should take a walk together, or have a quiet time together for a cup of tea. A part of your time together may be devoted to setting up the painting materials. Before doing the mirror exercise, be sure that paint and supplies are prepared with paint on palettes, water containers filled, and all supplies at hand. Each person should have her or his own palette.

When you have been together for a while, you can move into the painting experience. If need be, guide your partner through the usual opening breathing relaxation, and any opening ritual you may have selected or designed for this occasion.

Getting to Work

Do the following mirror exercise near your painting area:

➤Sit or stand comfortably, facing each other. One person must begin as leader, so designate person A and person B. Do the exercise in silence with person A starting off as leader. Your gaze should remain fixed into each other's eyes, so that you are getting information from peripheral vision only. Moving very slowly, person A begins to move, and B mirrors every action. The movements do not have to take up a great deal of space. Your concentration is to be focused on making a synchronized, nonverbal communication between partners. Continue this for a minute or two (never less than one full minute). When you feel completed, A comes to rest, but both people's gazes remain fixed. Then A designates, giving away the lead by simply saying "Your lead." Person B takes over the lead for another minute or two (these times can be longer if you like, but not shorter). When B is finished, he or she can bring all movement to rest with the body in the beginning position. You may do this exercise a second time.

➤When you are finished with the mirror experience, without conversation turn on the music and move to the painting area. Stand or sit side by side. Your bodies should be touching or close to each other. (You could agree ahead of time on a way to keep some physical contact. You can even hold nondominant hands if it doesn't feel too awkward.) Person A begins by making a single stroke on the page with whatever color and brush feels appropriate according to the mood of the music and previous mirror experience.

➢Person B responds by making another stroke with his or her brush in whatever color feels right. Be sure to receive the feeling and sense of each stroke before responding, just as you would an idea or comment in a verbal conversation. Continue the conversation, one stroke or movement of paint in response from each partner at a time, until you feel finished.

➢Sit together for a silent, still moment. You might want to change the music, share some food, or go for another walk. Spend some time talking about your experience and your feelings. How did the experience evolve for each person? You might want to do more painting or just follow a spontaneous mood.

This kind of painting can be done very large on a wall or floor, but I suggest that you do it for the first time on a table. If you do it as a wall painting, I suggest that you tie yourselves together at the waist or leg with a ribbon. I know this sounds a little crazy, but it's easy to lose the deeply personal and physical connection when you begin to work big, and being physically connected keeps the partners in tune with each other.

Healing

Creative Meditation has a healing power that can be helpful in situations of physical pain or in relationship problems. The partner painting exercise can be an enriching and transformative experience for marriage, family, or household partnerships. Creativity is a very intimate experience, and there is a deep dimension of communion among participants. That communion in turn generates ongoing mutual support.

Healing Relationships

A woman in one of my fall semester classes had always been extremely intimidated by the accomplishments of her very artistic mother, a graduate of the Chicago Art Institute. During the course, we did a process with brilliant watercolors that piqued her imagination, and she began to pursue the process on her own at home. One day she came in and announced to me that she was converting the potting shed in her backyard into a little studio where she could immerse herself in painting.

By the end of the semester she had created an entire series of abstract watercolors, and she asked me to help her select one for framing as a holiday gift for her mother. Her fears of rejection and judgment persisted, but she knew that this would be the final necessary step in claiming her own creative power.

Returning from the semester break, she happily recounted the story of her mother's delight in receiving the painting. This inspired her to upgrade her studio with some improvements.

I didn't see this woman again for a couple of years. I had learned of her mother's recent death when we met by chance at a lecture. When I gave her my condolences on the loss of her mother she thanked me, saying that the experience with the painting had brought them so much closer than they'd been through her youth. "I was able to let go of so many bad feelings I'd held onto for years. It really helped me to love her in a whole new way."

The most interesting aspect of this story is the fact that this woman's mother never engaged in Creative Meditation with her daughter, but that the daughter was able to carry the healing she had received from her new creative self-confidence into her relationship. This took a lot of courage. I remember the fear she had originally expressed that her mother's response would undermine all the progress she'd made. I think her greatest courage came from knowing that her creative experience was no longer rooted in pleasing anyone. She knew that what she had could not be taken away. She was certain that she could always return to the paint as a form of prayer and personal celebration of life.

One more story exemplifies the effect the Creative Meditation experience can have on a marriage. When I asked some of my former students for feedback and evaluation, one of them made a brief tape for me. Thanks to Jean Searles for sharing her story:

> I remember being very excited about starting the Creative Meditation class, and when I told my husband about it I was a little upset that he wanted to join me. I was afraid that the experience would somehow be changed by having the man in my life take part in the experience. I really wasn't sure how he was going to respond to the class, so at the beginning of the first meeting, I decided that I wasn't going to allow his presence to stop me from having a full experience. The ritual was a tremendous introduction because it gave you a mind-set. I was delighted to find out that it had been a wonderful experience for him too. It was really a kind of beginning for both of us.
>
> In the end, I'd have to say that the most outstanding benefit I received from the Creative Meditation class was the change in my relationship with my husband. We both looked forward to the Wednesday night classes, and would hurry through the day to get to class. It was such a release. It was like three hours of deep massage. You kind of massaged your whole being, your nerves. You walked away from your everyday responsibilities, and got in touch with another part of yourself. We've always had pretty good communication, and we've always had a good friendship, but by doing Creative Meditation together we learned to communicate in a different way with one another.
>
> In this society I think you have to guard the soft, sensitive part of your being because it's so easily damaged and attacked. But in the Creative Meditation experience we could expose that part, we could let people see the underside. The class became a loving, supportive group. A nurturing place. I was able to let a part of myself out, and John and I had an opportunity to see this in each other. And I don't think I'd ever recognized this sensitive and vulnerable side of him.

Personal Healing

It's important to recognize that even when working alone, painting can help shift the focus off of mental or physical pain by filling the eye and mind with color, line, and the constantly unfolding surprises inherent in the creative process. It's not unusual to hear craftspeople refer affectionately to their tools and materials. When we are working, these things give us companionship in an otherwise lonely time. You may already have developed this feeling through your own painting and drawing meditations. Certain brushes become favorites, or a certain easel or type of paper. When you go to these things, you feel a certain comfort, familiarity, and support. If you haven't already become conscious of this, spend a little time with your tools. Just handle them. Look at the paint marks and scratches. They may even have some teeth marks in them. Look at the floor coverings that catch the drips, and the rags that do the cleaning up. These are members of your creative community. They hold the spirit of your struggles and the joys of your ecstatic moments. Sitting in meditation with these things can be a powerful way to sink into the deep emotional and spiritual pool that is a constantly nurturing source for your creative expression.

My greatest lessons about the healing powers of creativity and the Creative Meditation process have come from participants in my classes. Here is a project that I hope will carry on the healing it was able to bring to Mary, a lovely woman who had taken my class prior to being diagnosed with breast cancer. I saw her some months after she had begun the difficult ordeal of treatment. "The chemo makes me so sick," she said, "but something I learned in your class has helped me deal with this whole illness.

"I can't find a drug that will alleviate the nausea caused by the chemotherapy," she went on, "so I sit down with a circle in front of me and I draw mandalas with crayons or colored pencils. Focusing on the circular design and patterns that develop is the only thing that helps to eliminate that nausea." Needless to say, I was pleased to have made such a positive contribution to her treatment.

The creation of a mandala can be a very intense and meaningful experience. Here we will use it to focus on the theme of this chapter, but it can be adapted to deal with many issues and emotions.

I first learned about mandalas while studying at the C. G. Jung Institute for Analytical Psychology in Zurich, Switzerland. Dr. Carl Jung had a consuming fascination for cultural anthropology, and his cross-cultural studies played an important role in the development of his theories. He traveled widely and documented important cross-cultural patterns in religious symbolism, practices, and traditions. Among these studies he discovered that the creation of circular design motifs was a common traditional prayer form indigenous to vastly different cultures. Such design motifs are called *mandalas*.*

---

* For further information regarding Dr. Jung's work on mandalas and other cross-cultural symbols, see *Man and His Symbols*, listed in the Bibliography.

Exercise: The Mandala— A Painting of Balance and Wholeness

In her book *The Inward Journey*, art therapist Margaret Frings Keyes writes:

> Jung described constructing a mandala as an expression of a self-healing process through which the psyche maintains its sanity and nurtures its own growth. This symbol, he said, finally contains the "innermost godlike essence of man." It stands for the deity as well as the self since it reflects the image of the godhead in the unfolded creation in nature and in man.*

To bring closure to this chapter on the social self, we'll focus this particular mandala on your personal relationships to others as individuals and in groups. You might want to add a dimension that expresses your relationship to society in general, or you could do a separate mandala based on that theme.

You have been questioning and exploring issues about your childhood and adolescence. Go back over your images and reflections to select four main elements in your social development. For example, these might be sibling rivalry, living in the shadow of a relative who was artistically successful, a traumatic experience in school, a physical handicap that you believe affected your relationships and your attitudes regarding your creativity.

Supplies

The form of the mandala is a circle. You will need either a compass or (the resourceful person's substitute) a dinner plate. (If you would like to do small mandalas in your painting journal, use a small saucer.) Other supplies for this exercise are

---

* Margaret Frings Keyes, *The Inward Journey* (Millbrae, CA: Celestial Arts, 1974), 58.

* Pencil
* Colored pencils, pens, crayons, or water-based paint
* Vellum drawing paper

If you decide to collage your mandala, you will need glue, scissors, magazines, and personal photographs according to your design and goal.

Getting to Work

➤Draw the circle on the page.

➤Within this circle you will have four cardinal points. These may symbolize anything pertinent to the topic of your mandala. On many traditional mandalas, these points represent the four directions, seasons, or elements. The essential point, however, is the center.

The center is the area around which the rest of the mandala revolves. For this mandala I will ask you to think of a symbol or image that could represent you in the way you relate to others. For example, a chameleon changes colors in order to protect itself by blending into the surroundings; a flag stands out in any situation, making a statement about what it stands for. Perhaps you feel a different symbol is needed to represent you for each of the four elements you chose from your reflections. You will simply incorporate these four elements into the place that would be taken up by one. Don't worry if you don't think you can draw the symbol you choose; just keep reading, and trust me.

➤Now that you have done the work of naming four elements, drawn the circle, and chosen an image of yourself, decide how you would like these four elements to revolve around the center. The image or images of yourself should be the focal (center) point of the design, with the four elements radiating from or circling that center. You could draw four smaller circles and contain each relationship in one, creating a quadrant that enhances or suggests the corresponding mental or emotional atmosphere. You may prefer to work with triangular shapes or other symbols. The mandala is a good way to learn to develop images as symbols and metaphors. Play with the possibilities in your mind and in your painting journal. If you feel that you cannot (I mean really cannot) draw your images, then do the mandala as a collage, or incorporate collaged images. You might want to expand the circle by putting a border around it, or by writing some reflections around the outside.

➢Make a series of mandalas if you like. You can base them on the same theme as this one or on other themes.*

➢When you are finished with your mandala, spend some time in your painting journal reflecting on the process and what the images have taught you. Perhaps you would like to place the mandala on, in front of, or behind your triptych altar as a reminder of the forces at play in your life. Burn a little sage or a prayer stick of incense while meditating on these images.

You are on your way to becoming a more fully creative person, a cocreator with the planet. With this altar and mandala before you as evidence, you can continue to celebrate the unfolding of the new you.

---

* For other ideas, especially for using the mandala motif toward the healing of opposing factors in your life, see Margaret F. Keyes's book *The Inward Journey,* cited above.

Integrity

Having moved out into the rich matrix of the social self, we come to the last element on our list: integrity. Integrity is best described as wholeness. This wholeness implies balance and well-being; it means that each individual is rooted in a confident self-knowledge that allows for mystery and change.

Think back to the Yoruba ritual and blessing in chapter 1. At that point you may have felt tentative about your creative potential. Now, after ritualizing, painting, drawing, and writing, you have a sense of your courage. You have seen that you can do things you never before imagined. You are just beginning to get a sense of your power. This experience of the integrity of the personal self is an essential component of the integrity of the social self.

The social self celebrates the experience of integration with the community. My social self, for instance, rejoices in the work we can do together through this book. This is a level of creativity I cannot achieve through my personal paintings. Integrity within the ring of society means compassionate behavior and honor toward all creatures.

The following exercise is a wonderful celebration of group creativity.

Exercise: Conversation Painting— A Group Experience

This exercise is a unique experience in confronting and letting go of some of the ego concerns that can be habitual pests. Some people treat their work as though it were so precious they don't want anyone else to touch it. Others are afraid to paint on a piece someone else started. In this exercise, everyone creates every piece. Be sure to stay with it until all the paintings have been worked on by all participants.

By the time you have shifted the paintings three times, changes will begin to take place. Do this exercise very self-consciously. Observe your emotions without judging yourself. Above all, have fun!

Supplies

* Tempera paints: primary colors, black and white, and optional additions
* Large, strong paper in individual sheets (standard weight butcher paper is usually not sturdy enough for this)
* Assorted brushes—enough for each person to have at least two, one flat and one pointed
* Water containers—enough for each person to have one or two
* Paper towels or rags
* Optional: any additional water-based drawing or painting media
* A watch: a must for the designated facilitator

Preparation

The first time I did this exercise, my friend Brother Joe Killikevic was the facilitator. I don't know if it was his original design, but I certainly thank him for teaching it to me. I suggest that you do it with at least four people, but you may also want to adapt it for work with a single partner. It works best if people can set up their painting areas in a big circle (the directions below will presume that that is the configuration used). Be sure to have the painting area set up before doing the preparation exercise. If you are the person to lead the painting experience and teach the Machine (see below), consider yourself the designated facilitator.

Some preparation is helpful for good group communication. I prepare people with a verbal check-in, a few minutes to hear from each person about how their day has been and how they're feeling, and an exercise called the Machine. The Machine, a theater exercise designed to develop communication and trust among actors, is an excellent preparation for this group painting experience.

For the sake of explanation, let's imagine a group of five people preparing to create a Machine. (If you have a group of five people, you might want to re-create the Machine following this example, and then create your own.) We'll name our group Yolanda, Fred, Yoshiko, Jack, and Tom. With the others standing off to the side, Fred begins by standing in the center of a cleared space large enough to accommodate the group. While each person will be moving, no one will be going anywhere. Thinking about the types of movements done by different parts of some complex machinery, Fred decides to synchronize the lifting of his right knee with the extension of his left arm. The arm remains at rest as the knee comes up to hip level, and as the knee lowers to the floor, the arm extends forward and up to shoulder height with the palm open. Knowing that he will have to keep this movement up until everyone has joined him, Fred makes the movements slowly enough that he feels relaxed in his pattern. As he continues, Yolanda comes in to join him. Studying the movements, Yolanda decides that Fred's open palm could be lifting something into place. She stands to Fred's immediate left with her elbows up pointing away from her body. Her hands are facing each other as if ready to grasp some round object between them. As Fred's arm reaches shoulder height, Yolanda mimes a movement of picking an object off of Fred's palm with her hands, then she twists her whole body to the left, "placing" the object on a spot that could be on an imaginary conveyer belt. She coordinates the turn back to her beginning position in time to meet the palm as it comes up again.

Tom, Yoshiko, and Jack study the possibilities of working into the Machine the way a domino player might survey his or her next move. They look at all the possible places where they could connect with a synchronized movement. Tom decides to join in by standing an arm's length away from Fred's right knee. He is facing the same direction as Fred, so he is not looking him in the face, but is coordinating his movement with the knee itself. Starting off with his arms outstretched over his head, Tom bends at the waist toward the knee as it goes down to the floor. As it raises, he begins an arcing movement to his right. The arc ends as the knee stops at the top of its lift. Then Tom returns. With his hands clenched, it seems he is grasping a round rod that is being moved by the knee.

Believe me, this is more difficult to visualize than it is to do. Let's recap: Fred's in the center, Yolanda's to his right moving toward the conveyor belt, and now Tom is on his left arcing to the right.

(Are we having fun yet?!)

Yoshiko decides that Tom must be pouring something out of the main piece of machinery and decides to sit on the floor just below his arc. Now each time Tom moves to his right Yoshiko, who is sitting Indian style with arms rounded as if grasping a large vat in front of her, makes three large circular movements to the right with her upper body.

Jack enters last at the spot where Yolanda is making her placement. As she returns to the right of her twisting motion, Jack takes up the "object" she has set down. Making a 360-degree turn, he stops briefly at 180 degrees to set the thing down before completing his turn to pick up the next one.

Once everyone is coordinated, Jack, the last person to enter, says, "Sound off." Everyone then begins to make the sound of their piece of the machinery. It all mixes together for a while. Sometimes people need to experiment with different sounds until they find the one that feels correct for their movement. When the sound seems to have become constant, Fred (because he set the basic rhythm of the machine) says, "Throttle." This means that he will begin to make his movement faster and everyone must watch carefully to move in turn. The machine then speeds up according to the first person's tempo. That person can continue to speed up if he or she wishes, which means that everyone must pay attention to keep the machine in unison.

After the machine has been operating in fast speed for a bit, the first person says "Brakes." Slowly he or she returns to the beginning pace, and then eventually comes to a stop. It's interesting to play with these speeds if you have the time to do so. Picking up tempo and slowing down really gets people in tune with each other in a non-verbal way. It's a lot of fun, and can even be done at a party with or without the following painting experience.

Getting to Work

Since everything has been set up ahead of time, the group can move directly to the work place. I like to give people a minute to sit with their eyes closed to get centered in their body, and let the Machine experience sink in. The designated facilitator, who is now in charge of the exercise, should have a watch, because timing is important. You may use music in the background if you wish.

Once everyone is centered and quieted, the facilitator reads a poem rich in imagery. Everyone begins a painting from the imagery in the poem. After ten minutes, the facilitator says, "Stop," and everyone is instructed to hand their painting to the person on the right. Before beginning to paint on this new painting, each person must stop to receive it. Reflecting on the Machine is a good way to get in touch with the kind of communication necessary in continuing each painting. Listening, watching, synchronizing are all words that now have a new application on the painted page.

You may or may not decide to tell people about this aspect of this exercise ahead of time. The act of giving up one's work, however playful the setting may be, is extremely difficult for some people, and it's not unusual to have some strong inner reactions. I have found that only after the exercise is finished will people share the intricacies of their emotional responses to the experience. Sometimes old memories are triggered and rebellious attitudes set in. Discovering these things is, of course, part of the process of the exercise. While this is a fun exercise, it acts as a projection mechanism for our attitudes toward working with others, toward our ability to let go of our own work as well as our ability to receive someone else's work. Some people are more intimidated by changing someone else's work than by giving up their own. In any case, it puts participants in touch with an entire realm of emotions that is usually not directly accessible. This is a safe place to encounter those aspects of the self.

Each person will work on each painting for approximately six or seven minutes. After all the paintings have been worked on by each person, they are returned to the original artist, who has five to ten minutes to rework the piece. When all the work is finished, allow time for discussion. Beginning in pairs before opening the floor to discussion makes it a little safer for people to express and explore their honest feelings. Most people are pretty open by this time to revealing parts of the process that felt painful at the start. Some people may recognize that they still feel angry or annoyed. Getting these emotions out where we can talk about them helps us recognize our beliefs about work and ownership. Some of us are sure we're not worthy of making additions to someone else's work, while others are sure that no one else is good enough, or has the right, to touch their creations.

Long after it is over, this exercise continues to provide material for reflection regarding how we see ourselves in society. It illuminates some deeply personal attitudes and emotions that may never have been brought to the surface before. The following questions are helpful in reflecting upon the experience:

➤Which was more difficult for you: giving your work to someone else or working on someone else's painting?

➤Did your feelings change through the course of the exercise? Can you trace their evolution?

➤What issues or elements were most important to you?

➤Can you draw parallels between this experience and any other situation in which you have found yourself or find yourself frequently?

➤What did you learn about yourself?

A friend of mine, Peggy McGuire, was fascinated by the prospect of trying this exercise with chaplains in a pastoral care unit under her direction. She asked for some basic guidelines and did the painting segment without the Machine. I was pleased to receive this note from her.

> I enjoyed facilitating "conversation painting." I was amazed that it went so well. Choosing the paints, paper, and music enriched my experience.
> I felt that some group barriers broke down through the process. The chaplains had fun and learned about themselves, each other, and/or how others perceived them in a playful way. They were able to talk about the experience of painting as well as adding to or ruining another's "painting in process" (or having their own completely changed). One of them said that being able to paint without censure opened up the expression of herself through color and form.

CHAPTER FIVE

Witness, Prophecy, and the Universal Self

WE HAVE CONSIDERED the realms of the ancestral self, the personal self, and the social self, reflecting upon the fossil-like memories of our personal evolution. Through the expansion of self-expression you have begun to bear witness to your life. You are growing into your artisthood, learning to articulate a unique response to the world. You are beginning to make choices about your paintings and drawings that were foreign to you four chapters ago.

As we continue our movement to the outer perimeter of the social self, the role of witness takes on a broader context. Learning to see and express our deepest personal experience is the essential starting point and the place to which we must constantly return for grounding and balance. The next step, however, must be to survey and reflect on the context within which our lives take place. I call this *contextual perception,* witnessing the situations and systems of which we are also a part. This aspect of Creative Meditation combines spiritual and ethical issues with political concerns.

Many examples from art history supply us with evidence of how artists, as the social self bearing witness to injustice, have given the world powerful images of the human experience. Picasso's protest against the bombing of innocent villagers during the Spanish Civil War is entitled *Guernica.* It continues as a powerful statement of rage and antiwar sentiment. The murals of Diego Rivera expose the corrupt structures of commerce and governments. Paintings and drawings hidden away by artists in Nazi concentration camps were later the most powerful firsthand evidence of Holocaust atrocities and the realities of persecution.

In the same way, some artists register a subtle commentary on their country and their epoch. Toulouse Lautrec, for example, witnessed the cabaret life of nineteenth-century Paris, while Mary Cassatt, Berthe Morisot, and Suzanne Valadon recorded the domestic life-styles of that period.

In his captivating book *The Prophetic Imagination,* theologian Walter Brueggemann defines the term *prophecy* and explores the Western traditional understanding of the term. Within this context, Dr. Brueggemann recognizes the political role of the artist.

Prophecy, says Brueggemann, is both critical and energizing, and in the legacy of the Western prophetic tradition, new order is always created from within a system rather than imposed from without. In our role, then, as creative individuals we must come to realize that the technical quality of our creative work is less important than the act of conveying our vision in the service of justice.

A prophet does not tell the future as if reading a crystal ball; a prophet is one who tells the story of her or his people by reading the events of the present. With a courageous voice the prophet speaks the truth of the time. A good example of a modern-day prophet is Jacques Cousteau, who announced to a naive world the polluted and tragic conditions of its oceans, and whose dedication to his cause has made the survival of the marine world a global concern.

1. Mandala *(Margaret Collis)*

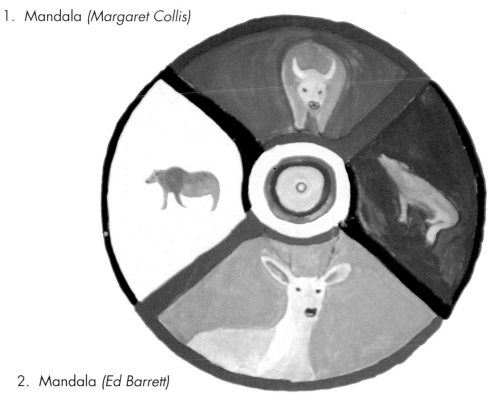

2. Mandala *(Ed Barrett)*

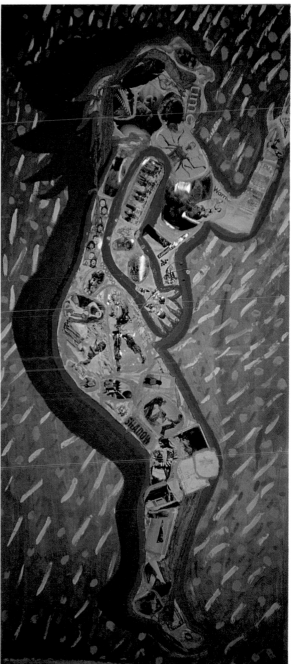

3. Self-Portrait *(Lynne de Spain)*, opposite
4. Self-Portrait *(Tom Tehan)*, above left
5. Self-Portriat *(Sue Draves)*, above right

6. Dream Painting *(Grace Blindell), opposite page, top*
7. Greening Power Painting *(Anne Estrada), opposite page, bottom*
8. Signature Painting *(Don Blaeser), above*

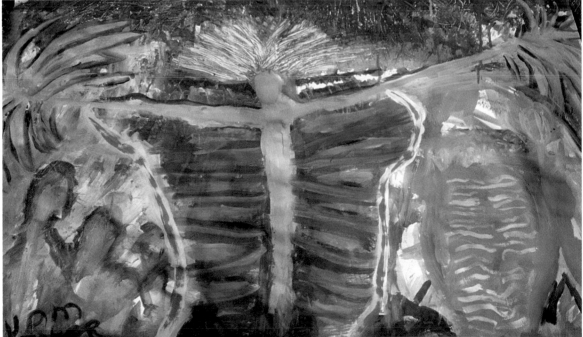

9. Signature Painting *(Yolanda Ronquillo), opposite*
10. Partner Painting *(Katie Green and Jennifer de Vries), this page, top*
11. Partner Painting *(Peter Worne and Tarquam), bottom*

12. Partner Painting *(Teresa Lee and Joelle Nicholson)*

Exercise: The Art of Reclamation—Developing Contextual Perception

Collage is the art of pasting, sewing, or affixing materials to a surface. The great thing about collage is that it awakens the artist and the viewer to the artistic potential of everyday things. Almost anything can be used as collage material. Paper, fabric, string, wire mesh, and found objects are commonly used. There are no restrictions regarding materials. Collage is an art of reclamation that provides a creative alternative for the use of otherwise discarded goods. From an ecological perspective, at a time when recycling may be a key to planetary survival, we could say that collage is the perfect art form for the ecological age.

Anyone familiar with the cubist period of modern art (1907–1914) will also have some familiarity with collage. Georges Braque, Pablo Picasso, and Juan Gris, three of the best-known cubist painters, expanded the traditional two-dimensional plane into a new way of expressing the three-dimensional image. As a part of their exploration, they glued and sewed various materials onto canvas, cardboard, and wooden surfaces. In the wake of this precedent, the use of such things as newspaper clippings, wallpaper patterns, fabric, labels, and string has become fully acceptable in the expression of social and political commentary.

Picture yourself as a pebble tossed into a river. The rings around the pebble represent the spheres of influence within which you live. If we look at these rings in terms of environment, we can consider our home, our street, our community, city, state, nation, continent, and planet. If we consider people in our lives, we might begin with partner or mate and go on to family, friends, neighbors, fellow citizens, race, gender, and species. Any and all of these connections can be focal points or catalysts for our artistic images. In the collage projects in this chapter we will be using collected objects as a way of creating editorialized portraits of our environments.

I think you will find collage a very freeing experience. If you loved cutting and pasting when you were a kid, if you kept a scrapbook, you'll love collage. People who are still hooked on making something look "like it's supposed to" usually love collage, too, because it allows the use of drawings and photographs from other sources. If you did some gluing and pasting in your self-portrait, you have an idea of how a collage can look.

We're going to do three collage projects; the first one is entitled "Home." It is a collage created from things you find in the place you live, and it serves as an effective tool for developing contextual perception.

Supplies

Supplies are essentially the same for all three projects; see resource 1 for explanations and information.

* "Stuff" collected from your garbage, your pockets, purse, wallet, dresser, and so on. Here's a list of possible stuff: soap wrappers, dog fur, paw prints, shopping lists, snapshots, envelopes, letters, canceled stamps, concert tickets, lipstick-blotted tissue, clothing labels, sections of bills or canceled checks, doodles, phone scribbles, old calendar pages, labels from favorite foods, sales tags, old church bulletins, hair, one-of-a-kind jewelry, business cards, dental floss, hair ribbon, ornaments, keys, souvenirs.
* Sturdy paper or cardboard
* Polymer medium
* Water-soluble glue
* Available media (optional, just have on hand for spontaneous use): tempera paint, crayons, watercolor pencils and/or crayons, or any other media
* Brushes (if you use your regular painting brushes with glue, be sure to wash and reshape them carefully)
* A palette
* Rags or paper towels, water containers

Part I—Home

I suggest that you collect "materials" (this is your new term for the little bits of life that get stuffed in pockets, purses, wallets, or garbage cans) for at least a couple of weeks before starting work. As you collect, study yourself and the context of your home environment. You may learn a few things that you had never realized before.

You may not use everything you collect, but you'll want a variety of textures, colors, shapes, and lines. During the collage process, you can alter your materials to suit your needs or emphasize a certain message. Here's a list of possible ways you can alter the materials at hand:

* Paint them.
* Cut or tear them.
* Sew them together or stitch on them (paper or fabric).
* Use pieces of an object only, or scatter pieces on the page.
* Trace them.
* Photocopy them (copies can be used in a hundred ways: colored, multiplied, enlarged, written on, used as background, used as a pattern).

Be sure that you paste your collage onto very sturdy paper or cardboard. Some of the finest collages of the cubist and modern periods were done on cardboard, so don't hesitate to cut up some boxes.

Getting to Work

There are no specific ways to begin a collage. You can just assemble your materials and supplies around you and go at it. If you want some guidelines to work from, here is a suggested approach.

➤Lay out all your materials and supplies.

➤With the large empty paper or cardboard in front of you, take a moment to do your usual centering and relaxation with eyes closed.

➤If you're planning to use paint, put your selected colors onto the palette. Put some of the polymer medium into a little bowl. (You don't want to contaminate the entire jar with paint.)

➤Look at the objects you have gathered and think about your lifestyle. What do these things tell you about yourself, or what would they tell someone else about you?

Whereas in many of the previous painting and drawing projects it was helpful to empty your mind while you worked, with this collage project it is important to continue your mental process while you are working. Think about the context of your life. By this I mean your relationships and the structures of those relationships; your work environment and the role work plays in your life; your living arrangement; your likes and dislikes; your priorities; your political and religious beliefs; your hobbies and habits; recreation; the dreams and goals that fuel your life. Keep bouncing the ideas off the images and textures in your hands. This intellectual, visual, and sensual combination accesses separate parts of your brain, enhancing the integration of functions. Consequently, an image may expand your understanding of something that had previously been ideological.

➢Lay some of the things on the paper, and keep moving them around. You can sketch a possible layout with a soft lead pencil. These lines and marks can stay underneath everything (visible or not), or you may erase and change them as you go along.

➢Keep moving things around until you get something you like. Remember that you don't have to use all the materials you collected. You may decide to do several collages from them instead of one (this is how a series develops).

➢When you decide on a place to start, you can attach your collage materials in one of two ways. Polymer medium is excellent for most lightweight fabrics, paper, and other such items. Glue may work best for heavier items such as heavy cord, wire, or found objects. If you use the polymer, remember that it will dry transparent and shiny (unless using matte finish medium). Remember, too, that polymer can be added to paint, making the color more transparent.

Usually a thin layer of polymer medium on the surface is enough to attach thin or lightweight paper or material; another layer can go on top. Push out air bubbles with your fingers. Have several types of brushes to work with, and keep them wet to ensure that nothing dries between the bristles. (Acrylic media dry quickly, so be careful.)

➢As soon as one or two things have gone down, you will get a feel for something developing. Don't let negative voices stop you. Remember that you can paint over, tear off, and add to this piece. Think in terms of working in layers. Objects can go on top of each other, or colors can be painted on top of words, revealing provocative or cryptic letters. The more collage you do, the more you will feel at home with the process.

➢Above all, whenever in doubt, use the old "yes, and . . . " philosophy: I accept what is here and I now move on to see what will come next. If you have a question such as "I wonder if it's okay if I . . . ?" presume that the answer is yes. Throw dirt on the whole thing or sand if you want to. When that dries, if you want to paint it and glue some of your hair to it, that's fine too!

➢This is probably the only don't: don't try to be neat. Neatness is so predictable! Ugh! Let go and . . . enjoy!

When you are finished with this piece, look at it for several days. Ask yourself what new things you have learned about yourself and your home. What unexpected things have you learned from the collage? What surprises did you find?

In the next collages, I am going to ask you to extend the project you did in your home to your neighborhood and your city. Before you embark upon these projects, however, I'd like you to take some time to envision what such a collage might have looked like ten years ago (presuming you have known the same places for ten years). For many people, this may be a very sad project. Many once-prosperous American cities are suffering the disastrous consequences of financial, political, and social decay. At the same time some areas have become prosperous beyond belief as the new centers of growing industry, commerce, or trade. In either case, neighborhoods have undergone enormous change in the past ten years. What do you imagine would have been your commentary on the places you lived in ten years ago, versus today?

When you are finished with the neighborhood and city collages, I hope you will keep them as a sort of time capsule, to be brought out in five to ten years. You might also consider doing this kind of collage for other significant places in your life.

Part II—The Neighborhood

The process for this collage is the same as above except that you will need to walk around your neighborhood to collect materials.

As a student teacher preparing to teach elementary school, I was instructed to spend time walking around the neighborhood of any school in which I was planning to teach. This, I was told, was the only way to really understand the children who would be depending on me for an education. That was some of the best advice I was ever given in teacher education, because it gave me the message that not only was I going to be learning something from teaching, but that the children and their entire communities would be my instructors.

When you walk around a place, the earth speaks to you as well as the people. The trees, the pitch of the ground beneath you, the types of plants growing, the temperature; all these things are important information. The air, in sounds and odors, tells you about people, industry, cultural traditions, and language.

In a time when people are so mobile, we seem not to spend a lot of time in our own neighborhoods. If we commute to work, we suffer from being auto-bound. Do we know anything as well as the dashboard of our car? We're away from our home five or six days out of the week, and when we are home we're either off doing errands, cleaning house, working in the yard, or trying to relax. There's really not a lot of time for neighborhoods anymore. What do you know about your particular community? When was the last time you just walked around? Do you know the history of the area you live in? Do you know its smells, its sounds, its flora and fauna? Do you know the people around you?

A friend of mine recounted to me his experience of moving into a new neighborhood. While watering his garden a couple of weeks after moving in, he met a neighbor. After inviting this fellow for cocktails the following week, he thought it would be fun to get to know everyone on the street, so he went from house to house inviting everyone to the cocktail party.

Once the party was in full swing, my friend realized that many of these people did not know each other. He had assumed that only he and his wife were strangers on the street; instead, he learned that even those who knew each other had not seen or spoken to each other in years. Everyone thanked him and his wife for bringing them all together.

You might say that my friend created a sort of living collage. While I'm not suggesting that you create your collage in that way, doing this project can expand your sense of home and awaken others to their own neighborhood as well. It may take a little more time to gather materials for this second collage, but the rewards can be more than artistically rewarding.

Materials for this collage might be:

* Objects found on the street
* Photos of houses, neighbors
* A map of your neighborhood
* Street names
* Leaves from neighboring plants
* Newspaper articles
* Home Owners' Association newsletter
* Autographs

Follow the guidelines given above if you need to. You may want to work a bit larger for this collage, and if you live with another person or persons, you might want to have everyone join in. Either each person could do their own collage or you could all do one together. In doing individual collages, it might be interesting to see if the focus or the character of the neighborhood changes according to the artist.

Once again, as in part 1, take some time to observe the nuances and surprises of this piece. Did you learn something new or come to some new realizations about your neighborhood?

Part III—The City

By this time you have a good understanding of the process. While the movement into this third ring seems quite natural, for city dwellers it presents some interesting challenges. Very large cities are impossible to explore completely. If you live in a metropolis like New York City, you may need to work from newspaper articles and headlines for some of your imagery.

Does your city have an image? Is your image of it the same as the popular image? How does it differ, and how will you portray that difference? Travel to some of the different areas of your city. Walk around, have lunch or dinner, go dancing, go to bookstores or record stores. What is the air telling you about your city in its many different moods and colors? What is the earth like in your city?

You might also want to incorporate your memories of the city into this collage, or make a nostalgia collage. If you are living in the place where you grew up, your feelings and knowledge of the city have probably changed a lot over the years.

This piece, more than the other two, provides for a variety of approaches. For instance, you may want to put images of yourself into this collage to parallel personal change with city changes. You could present the city within the theme of a Greek myth: What would Ulysses have encountered if his Odyssey had been through the streets of Chicago, for instance?

The choice of found objects in this project can become a crucial element. Certain objects carry greater emotional or intellectual impact than others. Objects have the power to bring together thought and feeling in a way that language cannot. Coming to recognize such objects and learning to use them in your work can add force to the ideas you want to convey.

Take your time with this project. It is meant to be more than a singularly spiritual experience. The city collage is more intellectual and political than any of the other projects. The collage process forces us to open our eyes and see what is around us as if we have never seen it, even though it was never hidden.

Look around and learn about your environment with new eyes. Society is counting on the artist to produce work that makes visible the unseen. Art is a mirror, the self-revelation of society. We must have the courage to articulate images that are keenly perceptive and honest. A creative act is one that pushes past the existing state of affairs. History teaches us that individual visions and goals can become the reality of whole societies. Cultural evolution is the accumulation of the aspirations and accomplishments of those individuals who combined their power to imagine with the courage to create. This is the power of the people to create a future beyond the proscriptions of systems and encultured injustice.

The cultivation of imagination is a constant component of the Creative Meditation process. If you have played along, you can now see the proof of your own creative abilities. You have only begun to experiment with your "talents," yet you are capable of creating things you never thought possible.

What was keeping you from discovering your creativity? What was standing in the way of your imagination? I hope that by now you have shed any self-deprecating images with which you began this work. That self-deprecation is subtly infused by systems of education, religion, politics, and commerce. You are a fully creative human being, the animal privileged to possess the gift of imagination, which is also the gift of prophecy. Walter Brueggemann writes:

> Our culture is competent to implement almost anything and to imagine almost nothing. . . . It is the vocation of the prophet to keep alive the ministry of imagination, to keep on conjuring and proposing alternative futures to the single one the king wants to urge as the only thinkable one.*

Creativity grants us the opportunity to tell our stories, show our pictures, and sing our songs to generations of successors. This is as much the political aspect of creativity as it is the spiritual. As we realize the scope of our world citizenship, the contextual perception that we've begun to develop on a personal level becomes social analysis and commentary when pushed into the historical and evolutionary dimensions of human endeavor.

---

* Walter Brueggemann, *The Prophetic Imagination* (Philadelphia: Fortress Press, 1978), 45.

The Universal Self

The final ring of Creative Meditation pertains more to an understanding about existence than to an expression of it. It is the outer ring because it is usually the most mature level of our awareness, coming to us sometimes only in the last moments of our life, if at all. It speaks to the mystery of life and death and is more about space than matter.

Let's look first at the importance of space in the body. The body is made up of many elements: tissue, bone, cartilage, blood, and so on. Just as important, though, are the spaces within the body: the delicate pockets for air in the lungs, the pores in skin and bone, the hollow airway of the trachea, the esophagus. The first person who made me aware of this spatial aspect of our existence was my college biology professor, Dr. Groody, who referred to the body as a doughnut.

The spaciousness of the human form can also be considered from the perspective of physics. When we consider our atomic structure, we are made aware of our life as a community of dynamic atoms with their neutrons, protons, and electrons dancing through the biosphere. Light particles are bouncing, sound waves are moving through us—not to mention the molecules of physical elements that pass through us on a daily basis. When I listen to physicists I'm always amazed that we have any mass at all!

Now let's consider what happens to this body when it dies. It slowly decomposes, which means more and more space! We become the body of space. While we are material manifestations of the ancestral self, recycled a billion times, the universal self is space, the space within us, the space we occupy, and the space we become. To understand this we must accept this paradox: the universal self is the I that is not I. The universal self is timeless; it is the part of me that is already a part of all else. The universal self is existence beyond intellect and body.

The universal self gives us the wisdom of our space, which is the knowledge of connectedness. We recognize that we are connected not only to other humans, but to trees and whales and wolves. All things share the space. Just as we know that the personal self will sail only in the river of this lifetime, we know that the universal self will sail far greater oceans. The divinity at our core flows into the divine energy that embraces us, and we return home as a drop of rain to the holy sea from which it was born.

When we try to pick out anything by itself, we find it hitched to everything else in the universe.

JOHN MUIR

Zen and the Universal Self

In chapter 3, as a discipline of drawing practice you were encouraged to become "empty-headed," which is also an exercise in humility. Sometimes when we feel embarrassed by our ignorance we may try to make up for it or cover it up, but there is no reason for such embarrassment.

Let's apply our discussion about space in the body to mental space. A vacant space is a place waiting to be filled; it is a hospitable space. This is the kind of mental space we began with as children, when we were beginners at everything. Zen Buddhism refers to this "beginner's mind" as an attitude that celebrates ignorance as a clean slate, a nonjudgmental starting point. With "beginner's mind" we can let go of our anxieties and our expectations; we can relax our ego. By honoring our ignorance we open the doors of our perception and let all things become our teachers, just as in drawing practice. Occasions that bring us face to face with our ignorance (travel, foreign languages, new relationships) can bring on varying degrees of anxiety, because as adults we become ego-invested. We have a need to be "together," look cool, calm, and collected, or stay on top of things. With "beginner's mind" we can remain calm and collected, but we do so with a receptive and humble attitude.

Instead of doing some exercise to illustrate the universal self, I suggest you sit somewhere and do nothing at all except meditate on the spaces in you. Feel your emptiness.

On another occasion sit somewhere and think about all the ignorance that is in you. Celebrate all the things you don't know. This is a meditation on mystery. We are always on the receiving end of the universe until our creativity activates the energy that results in our gift. We are constantly learning, and every blade of grass is our teacher. The wisest sage is the eternal student, the one who embraces ignorance as a vessel always ready to be filled.

The lessons of the universal self are important to consider as you move into our final chapter and prepare to continue Creative Meditation on your own. The relaxation and surrender that come from reconnecting with your spaciousness rather than your fullness will help you past times of frustration and self-criticism. We can surrender to our ignorance with joy, and begin to pay attention to the information we are getting firsthand from the world around us.

In chapter 3 we embraced the beauty of Rainer Maria Rilke's poem "The Panther." The more I read this incredible piece, the more I am struck by the presence of the poet, sitting for hours as witness to the tragic captivity of that elegant beast. The intimacy of the portrait pulses with the immediacy of the animal's anguish. Rather than maintaining the safe distance of his human identity, after the first stanza the poem reads as if the poet climbed into the cage himself. He comes to know the pacing pattern and rhythm that "circles down to the tiniest hub." Penetrating beyond

For the momentous truth is that the spirit, the Tao, the divine reality must not be sought as something far away, separate from us, in a heaven to which we may ascend only after death; but rather as something close at hand, forever, and forever in the inmost of us: "more interior to us," as Thomas Aquinas says, "than we are to ourselves." Thus the holiness of life is not a kind of attribute but inherent in the divine nature of the ground, the divine spirit of man.

JOHN LANE

mere observation, he allows the animal to tell its story through him. His is a poem about the experience of imprisonment rather than the spectacle of it.

The eloquent articulation of that imprisonment not only connected Rilke with the panther, it connects Rilke and the panther to us. The poet is not just telling us the story of one panther; he is using the panther's experience to tell our story as well. The compassion we feel does not come from a metaphor in this poem, rather it is the result of the panther's reflection of our own despair. Whether we connect with the experience of entrapment, or celebrate our freedom by contrast, the poet dissolves the barrier between human and animal.

Most of us have stood in front of a zoo cage, as Rilke did, watching with sincere curiosity and wonder. Looking at the face, the teeth, and the claws of some exotic beast, our first response may have been gratitude for the protection the cage afforded us, and the leisure to continue our observation until satisfied. As artists, however, we must go deeper. A superficial encounter with life does not feed a muse's hunger, and Rilke was not himself satisfied with surfaces. Whenever truth is our goal, we must be ready to mine the source. This is the challenge to all artists, not only to bear witness to the world through communion with it, but to speak the voice of the great chaos as well as the great order of things.

We know that what we observe outside of ourselves is also a manifestation of who we are. Rilke went into the depth of his own experience and in so doing gave us evidence of the communion that takes place when a person is so receptive to the world that the individual story becomes a universal story. By having the courage of our individual self-expression, we bear witness to the whole of life.

And if only we arrange our life in accordance with the principle which tells us that we must always trust in the difficult, then what now appears to us as the most alien will become our most intimate and trusted experience. Perhaps all the dragons in our lives are princesses who are only waiting to see us act, just once, with beauty and courage. Perhaps everything that frightens us is, in its deepest essence, something helpless that wants our love.

RAINER MARIA RILKE

CHAPTER SIX

The January Time

*b*EYOND THE REALM of the rings, we are once again returned to our origin: divinity itself. Eckhart would have referred to our furthest point of divinity as the Godhead. I prefer to allow each person to name the divinity for him- or herself. Of greatest importance to the concept of Creative Meditation is the recognition of this life as the receptor and manifestation of the constant flow of the sacred creative force. St. Hildegard named it, Dylan Thomas named it, Lao-Tse named it.

In certain traditions such as the Yoruba or Greek, pantheons of gods are named to honor all of the many facets of the divine. This last chapter is named for one such divine persona, the Greek god Janus, who had two faces: one face looked back at where he had been, the other looked forward to where he was going. From this god comes the name for the month of January. So I have named this the January Time, because it is time for us to reflect on all that you have done thus far and look forward to doing in the future.

Just as you might reminisce over vacation photographs and memorabilia, plan a period of time to sit quietly with your painting journal, your private writing, and the personal memories of your creative work sessions. Did you ever get carried away and paint the walls, or someone's T-shirt? Did someone buy you a special gift for your creative work?

The reservoir of events you now have associated with the Creative Meditation experience make up a personal treasury from which you can draw inspiration and affirmation at any time. If something negative happened, keep it as a reminder of the importance of determination. We all must learn to deal with setbacks and people who may be threatened by our empowerment. Keep your resolve, and allow all the good memories in your treasury to encourage you toward a continuously creative life.

In reflecting on your work we will look at two aspects: (1) the paintings, drawings, and projects and (2) the personal interior evolution you have gone through with the use of meditations, visualizations, and reflection questions. Let's begin by doing a retrospective exhibit of your work. (You don't have to invite an audience—this exhibit is just between you and me.)

Exercise:
Retrospective

Looking at pictures can be as much of a meditation as making them, and certainly as educational. Your accumulated work in painting, drawing, and mixed media now gives you an experiential foundation for looking at pictures, and I'd like to strengthen that foundation with some philosophical and technical parameters.

Supplies

All the work you have done since beginning this book.

How to Proceed

Lay out everything you have done since beginning the Creative Meditation process. Don't be afraid that we're going to criticize it and tear it apart—we're not going to do that. I'd like you to feel grateful and proud of every painting. These pieces are your teachers and guides, and the ones you don't like can teach as much as or more than the ones you like.

Another quote from Rainer Maria Rilke provides us with solid advice:

Works of art are of an infinite solitude, and no means of approach is so useless as criticism. Only love can touch and hold them and be fair to them.—Always trust yourself and your own feeling, as opposed to argumentations, discussions, or introductions of that sort; if it turns out that you are wrong, then the natural growth of your inner life will eventually guide you to other insights. Allow your judgments their own silent, undisturbed development, which, like all progress, must come from deep within and cannot be forced or hastened. Everything is gestation and then birthing. To let each impression and each embryo of a feeling come to completion, entirely in itself, in the dark, in the unsayable, the unconscious, beyond the reach of one's own understanding, and with deep humility and patience to wait for the hour when a new clarity is born; this alone is what it means to live as an artist: in understanding as in creating.*

The body of work you have created presents you with two considerations: the process of Seeing the work yourself and the possibility of sharing it with others. Both private and personal exhibition will expand your experience of being a painter. Your own responses will change with time; be gentle to yourself. If you choose to show your work to others, be prepared for a vast range of responses. It is very important that you remember this: each person brings a uniquely personal history and level of sophistication to the work. You are not responsible for their projections and observations. It has taken me a long time to learn this, and after years of gritting my teeth while my work becomes a psychic trampoline, I can say that the more you relax and remove yourself from the responses of others, the happier you will be. (You might want to write this on a three-by-five card as a reminder.)

---

* Rainer Maria Rilke, *Letters to a Young Poet,* translated and with a foreword by Stephen Mitchell (New York: Vintage Books, 1987), 23–24.

Dealing with Response and Opinion

We need to ride our images as one would ride a giant eagle soaring up and down wherever they take us . . . our creativity does not consist in being right all the time but in making of all our experiences, including the apparently mistaken and imperfect ones, a holy whole. . . . Who knows what lies behind and beyond our images until we trust them enough to ride them fully, even into the darkness and into the depths like a seed in the soil?

MATTHEW FOX

Developing the discipline of creative work teaches us that becoming a responsible witness to art also requires preparation. Most people don't realize this. I have heard people standing in front of masterpieces of modern art ask in rhetorical arrogance, "What am I supposed to get from this?" The assumption is that the artist missed the mark because this person cannot easily read any meaning from the work. It is hard to explain that in order to "get" something a person must be ready to give something to the piece. This is not so much a question of learned educational information, though some acquaintance with art history is helpful. It is more a matter of a spiritual willingness to receive from and to be led by the work.

In her widely read book *Philosophy in a New Key*, philosopher Suzanne K. Langer addresses the problems of intellectualism and materialism as barriers to receiving and understanding art.

> The worst enemy of artistic judgment is literal judgment which is so much more obvious, practical, and prompt that it is apt to pass its verdict before the curious eye has even taken in the entire form that meets it. Not blindness to "significant form," but blindedness, due to the glaring evidence of familiar things, makes us miss artistic, mythical, or sacred import. This is probably the source of the very old and widespread doctrine that the so-called "material world" is a curtain between humanity and a higher, purer, more satisfying Truth.*

In dealing with others, try to remain grounded in the knowledge and satisfaction of your own process. Listen for constructive suggestions. Deflect the thoughtless comments that may come your way through ignorance or envy. Be generous with simple explanations that might help someone to understand. Many people feel very uncomfortable around art, because they don't know what to say. If you give them a safe and hospitable place to ask questions, you may reap the rewards of their fresh viewpoint and honest responses.

Seeing Questions

Learning how to look at paintings is important for two reasons. First, we need to learn how to follow the progression of our own work; and second,

---

* Suzanne K. Langer, *Philosophy in a New Key: A Study in the Symbolism of Reason, Rite, and Art* (New York: New American Library, 1951), 223.

we want to get as much as possible from experiencing the work of others. These two activities usually go hand in hand, nurturing each other. The more I study the works of other painters, the more I learn about my own. The important trick is to learn what questions to ask myself.

The best questions are nonjudgmental, yet probing. For instance, I once saw several Van Goghs in the Norton Simon Museum. With only a colorless photograph to look at, Van Gogh painted a portrait of his mother. The color he chose for her face defies naming. It is a mixture of yellow and blue, which I could best describe as celery or chartreuse. I stood in front of this small painting transfixed. It's as if he saw her with sunlight reflected off a colored wall. That color became the question, and I pursued it. I learned that he was taught never to use a flesh tone for skin. Nevertheless, his choice is still staggering, and the use of that color alone makes this a hypnotizing portrait, powerful and enigmatic. The leap of intellect it took for Van Gogh to create this portrait tells us something about his genius. His willingness to challenge the conventions of the time made his work a milestone in the evolution of painting.

Seeing that painting prompted me to reexamine prints of his other work, to examine more closely his use and juxtaposition of colors. When I look at my own work now I am constantly reflecting on my color decisions. While working on a painting, I often stop for days or weeks to study the work of the great masters. I recommend this even if you feel you don't know much about what you're seeing.

We must hold enormous faith in ourselves: it is essential that the revelation we receive, the conception of an image which embraces a certain thing, which has no sense in itself, which has no subject, which means absolutely nothing from the logical point of view . . . should speak so strongly in us . . . that we feel compelled to paint.

GIORGIO DE CHIRICO

Learning to Look at Pictures: Elements to Consider

The following brief list of elements is based on helping you look at the work you have done in beginning Creative Meditation. We haven't been concerned with the technical elements in painting or drawing, so the list is composed of the most basic aspects applicable to all work. You will grow in your understanding and vocabulary as you continue your work beyond this book. For example, composition is obviously an important part of painting that you may want to learn about as an extension of the work you are now accomplishing.

Turn to resource 3 for a fuller explanation of each element. It is intended as an easy access guide that you can refer to when visiting galleries and museums. Having read through those explanations, proceed to evaluate your work with the help of the following questions.

Style

➤ What word or adjectives would I use to describe my style?
➤ What elements contribute to that style?
➤ Do I see a continuity to my work? What creates that continuity?

Use of Medium and Materials

➤ What have I learned about the media I have used?
➤ Have I experimented with different media?
➤ What kind of experimentation would I like to do?
➤ Where is there an example of something that happened by accident that I would like to explore further?

Line

➤ How does line play a part in my work?
➤ Do I see a development of line in the paintings as well as in the drawings?
➤ Do I see different kinds of line? Can I see the evidence of having used different drawing or painting implements?
➤ Can I apply any lessons from my signature exercises to my drawings or paintings?

Texture

➤ Are there textures in my drawings? How were they achieved?
➤ Which are the most interesting textures? How did I create them? Did I realize what I was doing?
➤ How have I created textures without adding collaged or glued elements?

Focus and Balance

➤ Where is the focal point of each piece?
➤ Does the focus usually fall in the middle of the painting?
➤ Which is more interesting: a piece with the focal point in the middle (symmetrical), or one with the focal point offset (asymmetrical)?
➤ In the pieces with an offset focal point, did I achieve some balance with the other elements?
➤ Where does my eye travel on the page?

With the five elements above you can begin a dialogue with your own paintings and drawings, as well as those of important painters in the world of professional art. I suggest that you leave the work visible for days, if possible. This gives you time to notice aspects you might otherwise miss.

If you decide to show your work to others, you could acquaint them with resource 3 as well as the questions listed above. This will give them a helpful context for their comments, and facilitate a meaningful dialogue between you.

A Step Further: Composition Study

Here is an excellent exercise for studying the composition elements of a piece. You will need tracing paper (available in pads and rolls from arts stores). Using your own work or an art book (large coffee table art books are great for this—get paper size to match), and a soft lead pencil so that you do not leave any marks on reproductions, overlay a piece of tracing paper on top of the print or painting that you find especially intriguing. Usually you will be able to see only the major compositional lines and color areas through the paper. Trace them. When you lift the tracing page, you will have the basic composition of the painting. Look at the two side by side. On the tracing paper you can see the basic form abstracted to its organizational elements. Not only is this a good way to study how great painters created their work, but you can now carry this a step further. Working from the abstract organization, create your own painting or series of paintings. With the compositional elements worked out for you, allow the original format to inspire your own work.

It almost doesn't matter what you paint. It is what takes place during the act of painting that matters. It doesn't matter what style or technique you use. It is the artistic result and personal development that count.

The act of painting is a spiritual covenant between the maker and the higher powers. The intent of the artist flows through the work of art, no matter what the technique or style.

AUDREY FLACK

Turning Inward

Now that you have evaluated your work, go back and reread your written answers to the questions throughout the book. You might want to make some overall commentary on the changes you can now see, or you can go directly to the following reflections.

➤What have I learned about myself through the course of this book?

➤What new beliefs do I have about my abilities?

➤Have my attitudes about personal enjoyment and relaxation changed by learning this process? If not, what has stood in my way? Does it get in my way at other times? Do I want to get rid of it? Can I get rid of it? How can I get rid of this thing that stops me from relaxing when I'm doing Creative Meditation?

➤What do I need now that I am coming to the close of this book?

➤How can I get it?

Carrying On from Here

Though you are finishing your initial work with this book, I hope that you will continue to use it as a guide and support. Launching into the process on your own, you may have two very important lingering questions: (1) How or where do I begin without using the exercises already set up in this book? and (2) How do I know when I'm finished with a painting?

I've decided to let Pablo Picasso answer these two very reasonable questions.

> An idea is a beginning point and no more. If you contemplate it, it becomes something else. . . . When you begin a picture, you often make some pretty discoveries. You must be on guard against these. Destroy the thing, do it over several times. In each destroying of a beautiful discovery, the artist does not really suppress it, but rather transforms it, condenses it, makes it more substantial. What comes out in the end is the result of discarded finds. Otherwise, you become your own connoisseur. I sell myself nothing.*

I translate this to mean begin at any beginning and the piece will always go where it needs to go. Remember the dance: following, leading, balancing, losing balance, and regaining it. Regarding the issue of finishing, Picasso wrote:

> Have you ever seen a finished picture? A picture or anything else? Woe unto you the day it is said that you are finished! To finish a work? To finish a picture? What nonsense! To finish means to be

---

* Quoted in Herschel B. Chipp, *Theories of Modern Art: A Source Book by Artists and Critics* (Berkeley: Univ. of California Press, 1968), 273, 270.

through with it, to kill, to rid it of its soul, to give it its final blow: the most unfortunate one for the painter as well as for the picture. The value of a work resides precisely in what it is not.*

This quote may seem a bit more abstruse, but it is helpful to take his example as a guide. When we use the term *finished*, we are suggesting that all the life and energy has gone out of a thing or person—it is over and ended. A painting or drawing remains alive as long as its elements are lively. Without an instructor to see your work and give you some direct counsel about this, it will take you some time to make this kind of decision for yourself. You'll have to finish off a few paintings before you can gauge the difference between too much, not enough, and just right. A piece is "done for" when the image seems imprisoned on the page, when it has lost a sense of vitality. There is no scientific measurement for this; your eyes will grow to know it the more you paint, look, and learn. Have patience.

The last line of that quotation is almost like a Zen koan, and it gives us an opportunity to talk about addition and subtraction in the creative process. Now that you have been working and creating for a while, you have accumulated a number of pieces of work. Some of them you feel very good about, some you feel repulsed by (I hope you kept them), and others you are trying to figure out what to do with. The work in this third category feels unfinished and unsatisfying, but not repulsive.

It helps to keep working on a number of pieces at a time so that when the frustration over one of them becomes overwhelming, you can go to another one. I find that paintings and drawings teach me about each other. If I find a solution to one, I ask myself how I can translate that solution to another painting. This is not a foolproof method, but it is helpful. The important thing to remember is that addition is not always the solution. Sometimes you have overdone it, and the image cannot breathe. You may experience a sense of claustrophobia when you move into the picture plane. That is the time to decide what needs to be subtracted, and how best to do that.

When Picasso says, "The value of a work resides precisely in what it is not," I think he is saying that the value of a work is in what it evokes more than what it spells out. Constantly return to the spiritual source within yourself so that the expression has its own integrity and authenticity. Your primary responsibility is to your inner truth.

---

* Chipp, *Theories of Modern Art*, 273.

Learning to Be Your Own Art Advocate

*That is why art as medi-
tation is so democratizing
a movement: it returns
responsibility to each of us
for the images we believe in.
And with the responsibility
goes the fun.*

MATTHEW FOX

Now that you are in the closing chapters of this book, you may have to deal with others expecting you to be finished with the work. You may have trouble continuing to maintain its importance. How will you deal with this new challenge? In a way you are dealing with the original challenge you confronted when starting this book. Creativity is a daring act, isn't it? The personal challenge of continuing to be a creative and openly expressive person may have some frightening aspects to it. You will have to take time and space, and guard them from intrusion. Remember that our art springs from the knowledge of our weakness and the daring of our expression.

If you are to continue on this spiritual, creative path, you must continue to combine compassion for yourself with understanding for those around you.

Make clarity a goal of perception and communication. Ask for help when you need it, and be realistic in what you can expect. I have been in situations where the people around me felt philosophically supportive of my work, though at times their immediate personal needs kept them from expressing that support. You must develop your own inner strength and resolve.

Be careful not to set up unrealistic expectations. Be honest about the educational and childhood experiences you had. We have already looked at some of these, but it is important to expand your understanding to see how those personal experiences fit into a cultural system. Our work patterns and rhythms were set up according to someone else's instructions, usually a teacher (who was on a classroom schedule) or a parent. Unfortunately, most educational systems better prepare us to take orders than to establish autonomous thought or work systems.

Poet and educator M. C. Richards is an eloquent scholar whose writings deal largely with expanding human communication and creative empowerment. She offers some perceptive answers to our question in her illuminating book *Centering In Pottery, Poetry, and the Person:*

> Ordinary education and social training seem to impoverish the capacity for free initiative and artistic imagination. We talk independence, but we enact conformity. The hunger in many people for what is called self-expression is related to this unrealized intuitive resource. Brains are washed (when they are not clogged), wills are standardized, that is to say immobilized. Someone within cries for help. There must be more to life than all these learned acts, all this

highly conditioned consumption. A person wants to do something of his own, to feel his own being alive and unique. He wants out of bondage.*

Bondage: what a provocative word to describe the restrictions that impede our individuality. Over the years one becomes imprisoned by the patterns and beliefs learned at an early age and reinforced not only by educational systems, but by social norms and cultural expectations. The chains of this bondage are unfortunately strengthened by our own compliance and surrender to peer group pressure. What makes society uncomfortable with artists is the perceptive and challenging spirit they embody. At the same time, the creative dimension of every person longs for freedom of expression, and in some cases can only thrive vicariously through the works of others.

In her fascinating and helpful book *Internal Affairs*, Kay Leigh Hagan observes:

> The dominant culture of society does not encourage the knowledge of self because that knowledge cultivates creativity, independence, and defiance of authority. Instead, attempts to develop self-awareness meet with charges of being self-centered, selfish, obsessive, or indulgent. We internalize these messages at an early age, and by the time we are adults, the equation of the desire for self-knowledge with selfishness is hard to defy.†

The naming of this equation may be very helpful at this point. In order to have followed the exercises and projects in this book, you have had to make time for yourself and for the pursuit of something that has heretofore taken a backseat in your life, your creative expression. I want to give a round of applause to all of you who have taken that time for yourself. As Hagan points out above, we are conditioned to think that such an act is selfish, especially if it means taking time from other people. Making and protecting our own free space, our own work rhythms and styles can be a frightening part of the ongoing practice of Creative Meditation. Even though we are adults, we may be doing these things for the first time.

---

* M. C. Richards, *Centering in Pottery, Poetry, and the Person* (Middletown, CT: Wesleyan Univ. Press, 1962), 43.

† Kay Leigh Hagan, *Internal Affairs: A Journalkeeping Workbook for Self-Intimacy* (San Francisco: Harper & Row, 1990), 4.

Involving Helpers

By this time you have developed a way to meditate on your own. Use meditation to access some inner allies. In a meditation visualize, for example, a doorkeeper. This should be someone who is strong and determined to do his or her job. Talk to the doorkeeper about why it is important to keep others away from your work space while you are creating. Each time you do your opening meditation or ritual before starting Creative Meditation, acknowledge this doorkeeper and ask him or her to take a post at the entrance to your space. If someone comes to disturb you, the voice of the doorkeeper must come through you. It may be helpful to put up a note in the doorkeeper's voice so that a visitor can simply read it and not disturb you. It is helpful to state a time when you will be available. Creative work thrives on personal freedom and space, and no one else will claim this for you; you may have to fight hard for it.

Be patient with yourself. Work one session at a time. If an intruder breaks your concentration or your rhythm one afternoon, all is not lost. Resolve to strengthen the process of doorkeeping, and start afresh the next time. The same is true for every aspect of Creative Meditation. This is a slow and gradual process of reclaiming your creative powers. From the work of Richards and Hagan you can see that the hurdles you find in your path are cultural and social phenomena that you can grow beyond.

Exercise:
Reflection #4

It will be helpful to take an honest look at your personal environment. Spend some time reflecting on the following issues and questions.

➢*What is the social context of your family system?*

This question can be very complex, but to begin, deal with a few of the most important elements. The question will have a different bearing on you based upon whether you live with your family or alone. If you are surrounded by your family, for example, is there a sense of goodwill and harmony? Is there prosperity or financial struggle? Do hard times or hostilities keep everyone in a charged and unstable state? Many Americans are now aware of family systems, of dependent and codependent behavior patterns. If you are in such a situation, and you have had some counseling about these issues, you may already have some insight into the familial context of your life.

➤*How does your practice of Creative Meditation affect those around you?*

Can you be honest in looking at the ways others might be threatened by or jealous of your new activity? Have you seen any changes in your relationships since beginning Creative Meditation? Have there been any related changes in those around you?

➤*Do you see your life differently since beginning to paint and draw?*

➤*Have you made any changes to other aspects of your life as a result of awakening your creative spirit?*

➤*What are you threatening or challenging within your own life-style?*

Spreading the Joy

As you can see, there is a great deal of joy and spiritual healing to be enlivened through Creative Meditation, but awakening creativity can have its greatest effect when each person stretches her or his creativity to touch others, whether the others be individuals or organizations. This sharing can heal difficult situations and be a bridge between people. We can act as catalysts for the awakenings of others. Creativity is contagious. If your reflection above uncovered some potential problems within your home situation, sharing Creative Meditation with family members may be the answer to your problems. Once people see all the fun you're having, they're going to get curious and maybe even a little envious.

American writer Henry Miller, though probably best known with some notoriety for his novel *The Tropic of Cancer*, discovered watercolor painting in the 1920s. His dedication to it never ceased, and in later years he devoted more time to painting than to writing. In the delightful book *Paint as You Like and Die Happy*, the artist shares many of his insights and experiences. The following excerpt is a perfect example of the contagious nature of creative play.

> Some of my friends, catching my infection, joined me in these painting sprees. Sometimes a group of us would be doing one another's portraits simultaneously. And while we slaved away— "always merry and bright" we would discuss the painters we revered. During these séances we thought nothing of revising one another's work. The one who could do noses or ears well, or feet or hands, would doctor up the noses, ears, hands, and feet of all the others. We were learning in our own fantastic way, and it was fun. Now and then it was suggested that we get models to pose for us, but none of us had the means for such a luxury. . . . So . . . we would slip a coat over a chair and try to catch all the wrinkles, shadows, textures, herringbone effects, and whatnot. Or we'd do hats. . . . Coats, hats, shoes, whatever we fixed on gave us a kick.*

As you may already have learned from the work in chapter 4, the group process can be rewarding in many ways, and I encourage you to become creative in doing things with others even if you don't have an ongoing group of regulars to work with.

*Y*es, to paint is to love again, live again, see again. To get up at the crack of dawn in order to take a peek at the watercolors one did the day before, or even a few hours before, is like stealing a look at the beloved while she sleeps.

HENRY MILLER

---

* Henry Miller, *Paint as You Like and Die Happy: The Paintings of Henry Miller* (San Francisco: Chronicle Books, 1973), 78.

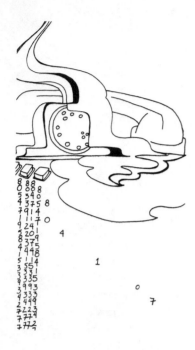

Above all, I hope that you will continue to practice Creative Meditation as a spiritual discipline. Toward that end I've drawn up the following guidelines to help you carry on your painting/drawing practice. If you are also interested in facilitating the Creative Meditation process for others, resource 4 provides guidelines for rituals as well as art exercises.

➤ *Continue working with a painting journal.* Keep the journal, pencils, paints, and brushes out where they will be used. Keeping them tucked neatly into a basket, drawer, or a knapsack waiting for a trip to the park is not the purpose of keeping the journal! (Keeping means using, not keeping for a rainy day.) Keep the journal next to the phone: if you're going to doodle, doodle in the journal. With brushes and paints nearby you can pour a little water in a cup before you start a lengthy phone chat and let the subjects of your conversation grow into painted images. These can be quick paintings, images that happen spontaneously. A series of such little paintings can be fun to revisit, or share with the friend who was on the other end of the line (they might even make a nice gift).

➤ *Use the exercises in this book over and over.* As long as you continue to dream, you will have inspiration for dream painting—even daydreams work. Conversation paintings can be done over and over with the same partner(s) or with new ones. Drawing is, of course, a practice that can be with you all the time, and I cannot urge you enough to give it ongoing attention. You may now choose to pick up some of the excellent instructional and inspirational books on drawing listed in the Bibliography. Using those books in conjunction with your Creative Meditation practice will allow you to grow in technical skills while maintaining the art as a sacred practice.

Painting from poetry is a wonderful practice. There are times when either through fatigue, confusion, or sensory overload I feel empty or internally chaotic. At such times, I go into my breath meditation to reach a level of calm acceptance of the place where I find myself. Then I turn to a poet for the counsel of images: Dylan Thomas, Marge Piercy, Rilke, Rich, Roethke. These poets and others have been wonderful companions through difficult hours, and I suggest their work to you knowing the healing and guidance they offer. Poets use a linear form to achieve nonlinear moods and atmospheres. In my mind's eye I see them blowing pictures into the air out of smoke, as one would blow smoke rings.

Poetry is truly a magical medium. One can paint the same line many different ways, capturing elusive images and allowing their transformation to take place through the paint. Imagine collaborating with Shakespeare,

Eliot, Dickinson! Such a painting practice is a wonderful follow-up to the exercises you have already experienced.

Self-portraits can be used in a more symbolic or philosophical manner, depending on what is happening in your life. If, for instance, you are going through a career change, you can do a self-portrait beginning from a stance that feels like a work posture. Collect images and ideas of your old work image and incorporate images of new personal and professional goals. Perhaps you are conducting a job search. You can collage the want ads that seem appealing, or ads that you have responded to. Incorporate your resume into the self-portrait. This way of looking at yourself may give you a fresh perspective on yourself, your past, and your future.

The mandala project is a very useful and adaptable exercise. Use this format for exploring the two sides of a difficult decision. For example, you might want to begin with one possible decision depicted on the right and the other on the left. Study the issues during the time you are drawing or painting the mandala, then draw a second mandala with possible compromises explored simply in the design. Ask yourself, Could this compromise work in reality? Try to push past your limitation on paper, then ask yourself if you have learned about real new possibilities.

You can also draw mandalas on acetate, a clear plastic available in art supply, drafting, or business supply stores. Acetate is used for projecting overlying images such as graphs. In the above problem-solving example, you might want to make a mandala for each possibility, then overlay them and see where they connect or can be made to work together. There is no end to the ways in which mandala designs can be used in personal work, not to mention the simple joy of creating designs as quiet meditation.

➤ *Keep taking creative risks.* Think back to when you started working with this book. Remember the risks you took to do your first drawings? You showed great courage in facing the challenge of the blank page, and it was your ability to throw caution and the opinions of others to the wind that got you past your earliest hurdles. If you subject yourself to external opinions again, you will lose control of your own creative powers.

T he important thing is to create. Nothing else matters; creation is all.
PABLO PICASSO

You may already have developed a technique or approach that you are very good at. Some people find that they have a knack for collage, or discover a facility for drawing. The more you recognize your own talent, the more you show it to other people. Their praise is a wonderful experience; those oohs and aahs seem to massage right into the skin.

The only problem with praise is that it can become addictive. We all love it, want it, and can get positively hooked on it. While praise is nurturing, a little of it can go a long way. I caution you not to let the praising

voices of others take over for the nagging, negative voices you exorcised in our first ritual. Paradoxically, all these voices have the same effect: they stop you from taking risks, dam creativity, and leave you with the same impediment you started with. If you feel you are in danger of such a thing, tell friends and family that you're playing with a new approach and you would rather not show your paintings and drawings for a while.

➤*Develop a new self-centeredness.* This self-centeredness means being focused on what is important to you, on what is your internal point of focus. Release your ego-centered self when you start a drawing or painting; move your energy outward from your core into the image. Begin to work with the image through textures, colors, and lines. Follow them to new, challenging places. Keep asking yourself, Am I following the flow of this image or am I contriving something? By contriving, I mean trying to come up with something. Cleverness is quicksand; remember the importance of authenticity and integrity. When things become too facile, too easy, or too cute, its time to push them into new dimensions.

➤*Don't try to continue this work without the prayerful and ceremonial elements.* I give this advice along with a little confession. Sometimes I go into my studio, put on some music, sip my tea, and begin to evaluate the work I've done in my last session. Before I know it, the brush is in my hand again, and I'm lost in the paint. It doesn't take long before I feel as if I'm skating on the surface of the piece. I feel ungrounded, and I become easily agitated when things don't go smoothly. Suddenly I realize that I didn't take the time to light my candles, center my breathing, and do my usual ritual opening. I drop everything then and there, because I know I will not be able to rebalance without those moments of meditation. In that ritual interval, I reconnect with the deep creative current. After years of doing Creative Meditation, the prayerful aspect of this process is still as important to me as it was at the beginning. Don't try to bypass it.

➤*Gather teachers.* There is an ancient Eastern saying: When the student is ready the teacher will come. If you have followed the teachings in this book and are still hungry for creative knowledge and experience, then you are ready for other teachers. Whether you enroll in classes or work from books, you will find teachers all around you. Look at the works of other artists. You don't necessarily need to go to museums or galleries to do this: the library is a great resource. We are fortunate to have excellent prints available in books and post cards. Study the drawings of Pablo Picasso, Käthe Kollwitz, and Egon Schiele. Study the color work of Henri Matisse, and the exuberance of Chagall. Study the traditional arts of native peoples from primitive times to the present. If you are interested in working from the human figure, look at bodies. Become a people watcher. Devour the world with your eyes, being intense and disciplined about your seeing.

The master teacher, however, is the medium. The paint and the pencil will continue to teach you about technique and about yourself; spend as many hours with them as you can. There is no substitute for the play and work itself. This is the ultimate advice for any person who longs to do anything: keep doing it.

➢*From time to time work with your nondominant hand.* Go back to each of the exercises in this book from time to time, and do it with your left hand if you're right-handed, or right if you're left, right? Right!

Here, in another excerpt from *Paint as You Like and Die Happy,* we can glean some inspiration from Henry Miller's enthusiastic reflections about working for the first time with his left hand.

> Thinking back to the year 1928, when I first began making watercolors, it seems to me that if I had not discovered this outlet I would have gone insane. My writing was getting me nowhere fast, my domestic life was a shambles, and my ability to panhandle had become nil. When I found what the left hand can do—"the left hand is the dreamer"—I became active as an ant. I painted morning, noon, and night, and if I ran out of paint I used crayons, pencil, or hunks of coal. (Coal on blood-soaked butcher's paper always yields something interesting.) Though my mind was intensely active, for I was seeing everything in a new light, the impression I had was of painting with some other part of my being. My mind went on humming, like a wheel that continues to spin after the hand has let go, but it didn't get frazzled and exhausted as it would after a few hours of writing. While I played, for I never looked on it as work, I whistled, hummed, danced on one foot, then the other, and talked to myself. . . . As if there were someone beside me, watching me, egging me on.*

➢*Dare to accept equally the powers and the weaknesses of your abilities.* This is not a question of humility or modesty. It is a matter of recognizing and honoring the sacred gift that creativity is for all humans, and celebrating the manner in which it manifests itself in you.

---

* Miller, *Paint as You Like,* 77.

In one of his beautiful picture poems, the courageous American poet Kenneth Patchen wrote: "Caring is the only daring."* Creativity must be daring. It must have the audacity to reach a hand into darkness and come out with a fistful of light. Creative Meditation is compassionate creativity. Art is the place where caring and daring come together. The creative person must not be afraid to take up space in the world, for in the ongoing courageous acts of creation we love the world into being. If the world is to be renewed, we must renew it. If the hungry are to be fed, we must feed them. If the darkness will be balanced by the light, then we will have to find and grasp that light for ourselves, to illuminate our own way.

This book is about painting and drawing as prayerful activities with transformational powers. When we look at the challenges now facing our species and our planet, it is not hard to see that thoughtful creative practice is called for on a planetary scale. Creative Meditation seeks to nurture every person as a spontaneously imaginative spirit in order to build a more reverently productive society. The Conversation Painting exercise in chapter 4 may prove to be the most important exercise in this book, because it encourages communal creativity and celebration.

In his fascinating and passionate book *The Living Tree*, English educator and artist John Lane affirms the prophetic writings of the nineteenth-century poet William Morris.

> If one takes the long historical view . . . the personal work of art, by the first quarter of the twenty-first century, will have lost its commanding relevance. As the dominant paradigm of art in western culture loses its authority, as the magical or participating consciousness replaces the rational, the old manifestations of bourgeois individualism, social realism, political propaganda and personal self-expression . . . will be abandoned in favour of more participatory, communal forms, emphasizing celebration, and the sacral mystery.†

Rather than abandoning the personal for the communal, we must value individual expression as a catalyst for communal activities. Private work of every kind must be encouraged among children and adults alike,

---

* This and many of Patchen's whimsical and provocative picture poems can be found in *What Shall We Do Without Us? The Voice and Vision of Kenneth Patchen* (San Francisco: Sierra Club Books, 1984).

† John Lane, *The Living Tree: Art and the Sacred* (Hartland, Devon: Green Books, 1988), 35–36.

because that work is the sustenance of the collective soul. In a society that is inspired by individual achievements, any infringement of personal creativity will be recognized as a diminishment of the whole.

The vision of an unprecedented movement toward communal art that is at once celebratory and sacred presents exciting possibilities for the future. The inherent affirmation of the ancestors is constantly urging us beyond survival to achievement.

Exercise: The Ten Commandments of Self-Affirmation

A couple of years ago while on a weekend retreat, I began to reflect on the Ten Commandments. I realized that as guidelines for living, they were now useless to me. Not only did they not help me decide what to do with my life, but most of them told me what *not* to do. The actions disallowed by the Commandments are not things I want to do anyway. I don't need a commandment to tell me not to kill someone, or not to steal. I doubt that anyone decides against murder or theft simply because it's written into the Ten Commandments. We honor our parents because we love them and they have earned our respect. Parents who have not earned that respect are not going to get it because of the Ten Commandments. Perhaps things were different in Moses' day, but those commandments are now most useful in teaching basic morality to children (and even children who don't get them can learn the difference between right and wrong). By the time we are adults, those Big Ten are common sense for most of us, and it's time we take the concept a step further.

Reflecting on the Commandments brought me face to face with paradoxical issues of obedience and autonomy. Rebellion serves us well in our early years. The desires and ideas of parents are a springboard from which to launch our own personhood and determine our own beliefs. Once the traditional rules and moral codes have been accepted or rejected, once a person has developed a certain behavioral mode of his or her own, it's time to assimilate the role of authority into the self. I realized that it was clearly time for me to determine ten commandments that would empower my own life as well as allow me to make a greater contribution to my community. One thing seemed certain: I did not need another list of restrictions and limitations. My commandments needed to be more than another list of "shall nots." I needed a list of affirmations, a source of constant support toward the achievement of my aspirations. Such a list could assist me in setting priorities and making decisions.

The experience of creating a personalized set of commandments was extremely gratifying, and I suggest it to you as a way of becoming your own authority and permission giver. It's not important to know the original Ten Commandments to do the exercise, nor are you expected to denounce the originals. Through this exercise, people of all faiths can create a personalized set of affirming rules. The value is in contemplating your life, the way you would like it to be, and deciding how you can empower yourself through specific actions and behavior.

Take time now or at the end of the book to do this. These commandments will not be etched in stone; you can change them whenever you want or need to. If you feel a "shall not" is in order and you are sure that you (not an external source) are determining its importance, then include it. A good example of a positive "shall not" would be "I shall not allow myself to be swayed into my old negative beliefs about my creative potential."

Here are a few more examples:

➤I shall make some time for daily tranquillity and centering.

➤I shall empower myself by learning more about financial things like investment possibilities or retirement funds. (Notice I didn't set myself up for a daily chore here, I just acknowledged that doing this is a positive personal step, even though it's not something I naturally enjoy studying.)

➤I shall love my body and work daily toward its health and strength.

➤I shall set aside some time each day for creative practice.

The following facilitation may be helpful for this exercise:

If you are near a hill or high place with a view from which you can survey a piece of the world in which you live, go there. If you don't have such a place, spend some meditation time visualizing such a setting. Have a pad and pencil with you.

Reflect on your life: past, present, and future. Think of the habits or behavior patterns that keep you from living your most joyous, healthy, and creative life. From this reflection, establish ten commandments based upon your own empowerment, the celebration of your spirituality, creativity, and the integrity of the earth community.

When you come down from your mountain, with dark gray or blue crayon make a decorative border on light gray drawing or construction paper. (These are your equivalent of Moses' tablets, so gray is best, but white paper will do.) Write your commandments on these sheets, and take them out to tell the people. Share them with at least one friend as a way of affirming these commitments to yourself.

Put your new commandments in a visible place. Read them daily if you like, or whenever you need a reminder of self-affirmation. My list taught me that within these parameters "sin" was redefined as a violation of my commitments to myself, and that my own empowerment benefits everyone.

This process can also be done in a group. Set a timeframe for individual work and designate a time for the regrouping. Design a celebration of the new commandments. Come together with food and flowers to share and tell your stories. The process that leads to determining these new commandments can lead to some powerful shared experiences among friends and family members.

Creativity: The Saving Grace

The alternative to living a courageously creative life is cultural catatonia. Creative Meditation is opening you to your transformative power, to the real magic of life: creativity. This transformative power makes every creative act a political act. Just as you are learning to play and enjoy painting as you did in childhood, you are also realizing that your creativity is a catalyst. The creative acts of the personal self inspire the social self to compassionate engagement with the world. Our self-expressive gestures are the responses of the inner artist, whose impulse it is to connect with the universal family.

As one who is called to spending long days and nights in front of an easel, I must confess that at times fatigue and frustration overwhelm me. The concepts I share with you in this book are not a Pollyanna philosophy. Reading ominous newspaper headlines and walking past the homeless on the streets takes me into the dark recesses of life's mysteries. I go deep into my soul and wonder about the significance of a life dedicated to bending paint into images. What is the meaning of painting in a world filled with violence and suffering? Always I surface carrying the same answer: the artist gives birth to society's images. The images we create are the collective host from which the human spirit takes sustenance, nurturance, and hope.

Our art is not concerned with museums or galleries or the auction block at Sotheby's, any more than spirituality is concerned with dogma. It is about the ongoing act of communion and transformation. It does not end when the painter sets down the brush; it keeps happening! Every time another person brings new eyes to a piece, it begins again. The Mona Lisa is a cultural icon of gentleness. Michelangelo's *Pietà* is a monument to the tragic grandeur of human sorrow. The images we create do not belong to us alone. Those whose creative spirits have not yet been liberated stand vicariously in front of our works, making their art through the strokes of our brush. No matter how much material wealth such a person may have, anyone deprived of self-expression is soul-poor, dependent upon us who dare to create beauty from which to draw breath, or provide light to shine into the dark corners of life. The soul-poor citizens live under a great tyranny, a self-imposed oppression of expression that is a form of dictatorship that no government nor Bill of Rights can combat.

We must also realize that creative receptivity is as valuable as creative action. Symphonies must be heard, novels must be read, and songs must be sung with people. Receptivity is not passive; it is an essential element in the life of expressive work. Our receiver role is as important as our creator role. Unfortunately, too many people focus their creativity on that receiver

It almost doesn't matter what you paint. It is what takes place during the act of painting that matters. It doesn't matter what style or technique you use. It is the artistic result and personal development that count.

The act of painting is a spiritual covenant between the maker and the higher powers. The intent of the artist flows through the work of art, no matter what the technique or style.

AUDREY FLACK

role, because they have no belief in their own power of creative action. The fact is that the more we create, the more we can receive. Our depth of connection expands when we have also experienced the fullness of the active aspect of the creative process.

An abundance of human endeavor must take us into the twenty-first century if we and the planet are to thrive. Rampant creativity must become a part of the human story. Creative Meditation is one more step toward a prosperous future.

Some years ago I had the following dream:

> I lived in a society in which human beings could have their atomic structure read by a machine, like an X-ray machine reads bones. Each person had a computer card with this atomic structure punched out in holes. Through the course of the dream I watched people go into a circular chamber, where this card was put into a slot. The doors would close and when they opened again, the people had been transformed into wheat.
>
> Common practice in this society was to have people and objects changed atomically, to make up for shortages and surpluses. People would be recycled like everything else, knowing that the system revived them in six months by restructuring the molecules of some surplus materials back into people. The system worked beautifully; there was no treachery or trickery, just interdependence, equality, and trust.

Waking from that dream I felt a great sense of freedom. First, it gave me another reminder of how interconnected life is, and second, it was a beautiful image of world peace and trust. I had no feeling of fear or worry that any creature would be misused or damaged by the system. It was an image of total cooperation and interconnectedness, an expression of how we are creating the world together. We eat each other in the sense that our work and our compassion feed people and economies. Our creative works may be concerned with any number of technical, aesthetic, political, emotional, or spiritual issues, but one thing is true for all of us: we are creating together the expression of a strange and unprecedented era.

The citizen of the twentieth century stands between infinity and oblivion, caught between the promises of the space age and the threats of the nuclear age. Living in a world community, we must recognize that we are called on to pool our powers of creative and prophetic work. We must become like Rilke with the panther, like the people of my dream: willing to become constantly new and other, willing to live in true communion with human and nonhuman alike.

New Renaissance

The Renaissance of the sixteenth century was a revolutionary period in human perception and expression. It was a time of waking up, a time of intellectual and geographical expansion. Authoritarian power was in the hands of religious leaders and monarchs under whose scrutiny the doctrines, politics, and personalities of art and science developed. The standards, philosophies, and values of this period still dominate the Euro-centered Western world, and our understanding of creative works, aesthetic and scientific, remain colored by ideas that are centuries old. Clearly, old notions must be redefined. Who can be considered a "real artist"? The academies and guilds of the Renaissance, which once answered such a question, no longer exist. Women and people of color, who were excluded from such venues, are now a growing percentage of practicing artists in America. The physically and mentally challenged are increasingly involved in creative work, and galleries provide space for their considerable contributions.

There is no longer a pat answer to the question "What does 'real art' look like?" As immigration changes the face of national populations, there is a growing sophistication about the traditions and art forms of others. Few countries today are as isolated as were sixteenth-century European countries. Our standards and ideas about art must be informed by the common ground of human experience. Art is about integrity and authenticity. It is about reverence, justice, and dignity. Art is truth piercing artifice. Art is beauty beyond material confinement.

I'd like to think that the period in which we now live will become a New Renaissance, and that through this New Renaissance we will leave to posterity a spiritual awakening to the sacred nature of creativity. Nuclear proliferation will turn into creative proliferation, destruction will be replaced by construction. Our descendants will cherish old family photos, the evidence of their own creative roots. They'll read about how we began to carry pencils and sketchbooks everywhere. They'll learn how we healed ourselves and our cities by painting murals together and sculpting monuments out of recycled materials. In centuries to come this could be written about as the time when art saved humanity and the planet; when as a world community we learned, for the first time, that the transformative power of the creator is in the people. "What a time to have been alive!" they will say. "It must have been great."

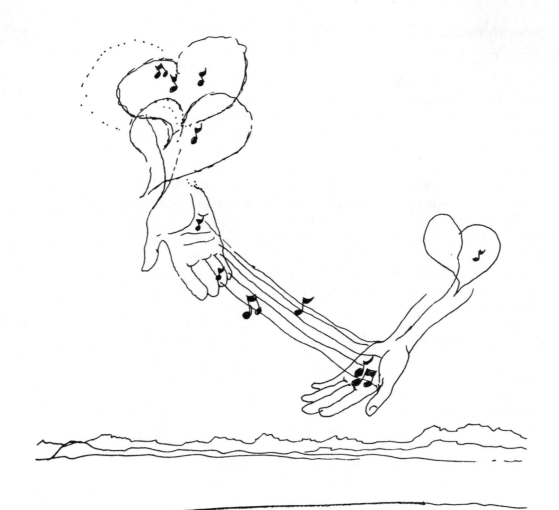

"One must love in order to believe in order to act: the best teaching, then, will be received from one who already has touched the apprentice through a sort of creative revelation that issues from the beauty of his own works."

Redon
P. 112

Supplies

THIS RESOURCE IS intended to help you understand, select, and purchase supplies. It will mean very little to you without a field trip to the art supply store. There, initially meaningless words will attach themselves to real things, and a whole new world will open up to you.

On the first trip to the art supply store you may feel like Dorothy on her first day in Oz. If you have a really good store at your disposal, the sheer volume of art and craft supplies can be a little overwhelming. Keep in mind that some of the greatest painters in history never went to art school and never had formal instruction. Art tools and media are definitely user friendly, and in this Oz every person plays the wizard.

The type and quality of materials you select may be determined by several factors. If you are working alone and have a reasonable budget for art supplies, you can select top-grade materials. But if you feel that working with a five-dollar sheet of paper, a thirteen-dollar tube of paint, or a thirty-dollar brush will inhibit you, start out modestly. All of the painting materials are available in a wide selection of prices and qualities.

Doing this work in a classroom studio, I am usually working with a somewhat limited budget; this may be your situation as well. Remember that the point of Creative Meditation is the spiritual fulfillment of the creative process.

While the artistic outcome of your meditation may eventually become an important aspect of the process, don't feel that you are required to pour a lot of money into it as you begin. Above all, don't use the cost as an excuse to push away creative challenges.

Here's my suggestion for approaching the art supply store. First, be sure to have enough time available that you feel leisurely about the visit. Second, take this book with you. Third, don't be ashamed of being a beginner. Go in with "beginner's mind." Be a tourist. Browse around, getting a feel for the place. Eavesdropping on conversations between clerks and other customers can be extremely educational. If nothing else, it teaches you which of the sales clerks seems most knowledgeable, and which you'll feel comfortable asking for help. Not all sales personnel have the same degree of experience, so try to get to know the staff in your store. Usually they will all work together, referring you to whomever has the specific knowledge to answer your questions.

Keep in mind that there are so many art and craft processes and materials that no single person can know the full scope of every technique or medium. For instance, oil painters may not be familiar with acrylics or watercolor crayons, while an illustrator may know a great deal about brilliant watercolors or gouaches but nothing about oils. So even very accomplished artists can be beginners in a new medium. Don't be afraid to ask questions.

You will also find a number of helpful books on the topic of art supplies, media, and methods. Such a book will be a valuable investment. I recommend Steven L. Saitzyk's *Art Hardware: The Definitive Guide to Artists' Materials* (see Bibliography). Saitzyk has put together a remarkably thorough and readable resource that will answer more questions than you can come up with!

After you have been in the store for a while, carrying this book while you browse and eavesdrop, open to this resource and read each section as you move from one part of the store to the next, acquainting yourself with materials. Each section will give you my recommendations for purchasing supplies in each category. I don't suggest that you buy everything at once. Take home a suitable sketchbook/journal and a few things that will meet the needs of the first few projects and exercises. After you have played with those for a while, you can come back to Oz and buy some more toys (by that time you'll be feeling a bit more confident as well).

Paper

Before making your initial paper purchase, take a look at the newsprint, drawing pads, sketchbooks, and watercolor pads. Feel the paper, look at the surface textures, and feel the weight.

Newsprint

Newsprint, a lightweight paper, is very uniform in texture and weight. Its smooth surface is especially suitable for sketching with soft lead and charcoal instruments. Sharp pencils will easily cut into it, and markers will soak through. Water soaks and weakens it very easily. Nevertheless, newsprint is wonderful stuff, and you should have one pad of it. It is good for drawing practice (you'll need it for chapter 3), and you can play around with pencils, crayons, and markers (watch the other side) without feeling that your playful images should be professional looking.

Size suggestion: fourteen by seventeen inches or eighteen by twenty-four inches.

Drawing Paper Pads

While newsprint is for drawing and sketching practice, it is not considered a quality-grade drawing paper. Good drawing paper is available in a number of different textures and weights. I suggest a medium vellum drawing paper. This paper is sturdier than newsprint; it will usually take a little water and many different types of pencil and crayon. It will not fall apart with tempera paints, though it may tend to warp a bit. (Such warping can be flattened by pressing the sheet under a heavy weight, such as books.)

Size suggestion: eighteen by twenty-four inches (larger if you like, but not smaller).

Drawing and All-Purpose Single-Sheet Papers

A good art supply store will have a separate department for quality papers. Usually they have books of samples (you can even buy small sample sheets). In the sample book, each sample will contain the name of the paper, what it is best used for, and the price.

In my classes I use a paper called Mohawk Superfine. It serves us well for drawing and painting, and it comes in large sheets, twenty-six by forty inches. This is an excellent size; if you can't find this exact paper, buy something of a similar size that has both a painting and a drawing capacity.

Sketchbooks

Usually, sketchbook paper is a medium-bond drawing paper, sturdier than newsprint, but not as high quality as vellum. You are looking for a sketchbook with paper that will take watercolor, tempera, pencil, and crayon.

Size suggestion: just large enough to fit conveniently into your lifestyle. It should fit into whichever receptacle you use most often (glove box, bag, basket, bicycle basket, or backpack).

Watercolor Paper

Like drawing paper, watercolor paper is available in many weights and textures. If you want to buy watercolor paper (it is not required for any of the projects or exercises as long as your drawing paper is sturdy enough) you should begin with the least expensive weight in a larger size, rather than heavy-duty paper in a small tablet or block.

When using watercolor paper from a pad, you should tape down the sheet (with masking tape) along the complete border. This minimizes warping. Using a watercolor block (a stack of watercolor sheets glued together on all four sides, with the exception of an inch or so of space at one place along the bound edges) eliminates this taping procedure, but to prevent warping you should leave the painting on the block until it is dry. Because of this need, the block can pose a limitation.

Butcher Paper

I encourage the use of butcher paper because it has so many creative possibilities. It is fairly thin, but it's strong and holds up well when exposed to water and various drawing implements. A number of exercises in this book call for it, so I suggest you get a roll at least forty inches wide. It's especially good to have on hand if you're working with groups, or if you want to encourage your household to become more creative. Just hang a length of butcher paper on an empty wall, and put a box of marking pens nearby.

Etceteras

Through your browsings you probably came across paper for charcoal, pastels, illustration, and even oil painting. Once you have a sense about the Creative Meditation approach, I hope you will expand your artistic explorations to a number of media and papers. You may decide to take a class, or to explore new things on your own. One way or the other, continue to follow the Creative Meditation approach to maintain a process that is non-product-oriented.

Gesso

Gesso is not a paint. It is a ground medium suspended in water that is used to prepare surfaces to take paint. Gesso is suggested for the preparation of the box to be used in the Triptych Altarpiece project; it is not needed for paintings on papers.

Gesso is painted on a surface before anything else is painted, usually in thin layers that are each allowed to dry, then sanded before the next one is applied. Any number of layers can be applied, depending on the desired final surface. The original consistency of gesso is pretty thick, so it is often thinned by adding small amounts of water and stirring into a smooth consistency. You will need only a small jar of it. Putting a small amount of gesso into a separate container (one with a tight-fitting lid), thin down the gesso before applying it in layers. Put on as many layers as you need. The more layers of gesso you have, the more impervious the surface will be.

Paints

This section is intended to give a little background about the many types of paint available. In the beginning it will be helpful at least to understand some of the differences between them. Ultimately, handling them and working with them will give you practical knowledge of their unique physical properties.

The following brief descriptions are designed to acquaint you with the basic differences in the water-soluble paints used in the projects and exercises in this book. For more detailed information, I again refer you to one of the resource reference books listed in the Bibliography.

All of the paints suggested in this book are water soluble. You will not have to worry about turpentine, oils, or varnishes. You'll be able to wash your hands and your brushes in warm water and mild dishwashing soap. If you get paint into your clothing, wash it out as soon as possible, before it dries.

Most of the projects and exercises are intended to be done with tempera paint, but they can be done in acrylic paint instead. The Breath of God must be done with brilliant watercolors or a similarly vibrant ink.

Finger Paint

If you have trouble finding finger paint in your art store, go to a toy store. Finger paint is not a permanent art medium (unless you get it in your clothes!), but it is great fun and personally educational (see chapter 1). The paper you will use for this medium should have a smooth and shiny surface. If you buy finger-painting kits in the toy store, some paper is often included. If you want more paper (which you certainly might), pick up a role of white, shiny shelf paper. It may be narrow, but the surface is perfect for your needs. If your art supply store has a large paper department, they may sell finger-painting paper by the sheet.

Brilliant Watercolors

Brilliant watercolors are actually a mixture of watercolor and ink. Unlike cake or tube watercolors, they come in bottles, often with an eyedropper top. The colors are extremely vibrant and do not fade when they dry. You might find them under the label of watercolor dyes.

Temperas

You may be familiar with temperas, or poster paints, from elementary school. While this is one of the lower-grade art materials, it is excellent for Creative Meditation for two reasons: it may help to invoke the childhood playfulness we're looking for, and it is so inexpensive that we're less likely to get caught up in the idea that we're trying to make art.

Temperas come in premixed plastic squeeze bottles. The current grade of temperas are a vast improvement over the old quality. You can find a good variety of colors, and while they still fade when they dry, the loss of color is not significant. I can't guarantee how they will hold up to sunlight, however, should you decide to display them for a long period of time.

You'll find that a little goes a long way, so squeeze sparingly, or you may waste a good deal.

Some companies now offer temperas in dry cake boxes. These are great for travel or desktop. They come in a wide range of colors, and I suggest that you keep some of these next to your painting journal.

Acrylics

Acrylic paints come in tubes or jars. They usually vary in consistency, depending on the manufacturer. They can be diluted and smoothed into any consistency, and unlike tempera paint, which will crack and flake if applied too heavily, acrylics will dry to a sturdy and lasting surface. They will not fade when dry, and they can be used even on surfaces that get a bit of handling, like book covers.

Acrylics are a durable and vivid medium. Be sure to keep brushes wet, because once acrylics dry they don't come out.

Polymer Medium

Polymer medium is an additive to extend acrylic paints. It comes in jars and is milky white before drying transparent. I have used it with temperas to add durability and prevent flaking. There are two types of polymer medium: gloss and matte. The first adds a gloss to the surface and strengthens it. If you add too much, however, the paint will become transparent. If you decide to use it, I suggest you do so sparingly.

India Ink

India ink is made of carbon and is waterproof when dry. Like acrylic paint, once it is dry, it will not lift off of a surface. You can, however, wash brushes in warm water and mild detergent as long as you have not allowed the ink to dry in the brush. India ink can be applied with brush, pen, or dropper.

Palettes

A palette is the surface you put the paint onto before you put it onto the page or canvas. There are many types of palettes on the market, and you will probably decide what feels comfortable for yourself. Most of the time you will not be holding it in the style of the stereotypical image, so you may not need a hole in your palette for your thumb.

When working with water-soluble materials, I find that used styrofoam plates work very well as palettes. For one thing, they are not biodegradable, and using them for art is one of the few ways of recycling them. (I don't suggest that you go out and buy them for palettes.) In the absence of those, you can simply select any other art store palettes available. A few China or plastic plates from the thrift store are also excellent.

While you're at the thrift store, pick up some old butter knives—they make great palette knives (for moving paint around or applying to surface). Palette knives in art supply stores are exorbitant and usually rust.

Pencils and Crayons

Pencils and crayons are great for working in the painting journal. But the work you begin there should be exploration that will lead you to using these versatile materials in conjunction with paint.

Graphite is the regular lead pencil with which you learned to write. But there are grades of drawing pencils, which range from hard to soft. The hard leads will have the letter H and a number before it. The higher the number, the harder the graphite. Soft lead pencils have a number preceded by the letter B. The higher the number, the softer the graphite.

I suggest you start with a 2B and a 4B soft pencil and a 2H hard pencil. You should also have a hand-held sharpener and a kneaded eraser (see below).

Colored Pencils

There are many types of colored pencils. Most of the major art suppliers make adequate-quality pencils in a broad selection of colors. I usually recommend Prismacolor pencils, which have a top reputation, and for good reason. They are a wax-type pencil with excellent color and are capable of creating beautiful surfaces. Remember that most color pencils are not as erasable as soft graphite.

Wax Crayons

While wax crayons are not considered a permanent medium, they are one of the best toys for creative playing. Having a crayon in your hand can take you back to your childhood muscle memory. I suggest that you get at least a small box of crayons, and use them in your journal.

Watercolor Pencils and Crayons

Watercolor pencils and crayons are a relatively new addition to the art supply scene. They are great fun and extremely versatile. You can work either of them the way you would colored pencils or crayons, then add water with a brush, a spray bottle, or your fingers. They can be used with temperas, acrylic paints, and/or polymer medium.

Kneaded Erasers

I don't allow my students to use any eraser when we begin drawing. The reason is that the presence of the eraser can evoke all the memories of making mistakes. Mistakes are teachers, the best teachers, and we should honor them as such. The kneaded eraser is eventually allowed, because it can play many roles. It is very gentle to paper, so you can do a lot of erasing without upbraiding the surface. When you work with the softer graphites, it is easy to smear and smudge the image; a kneaded eraser is excellent for cleaning areas around the drawing. It can be manipulated into any configuration. It can be pointed to fit into tiny places, or flattened to make large, sweeping motions.

The kneaded eraser can also be used on top of graphite or chalk pastels to highlight and blend areas. It is a versatile tool, and the only type of eraser I heartily recommend.

The Sandpaper Block

The sandpaper block is a small pad of sandpaper strips stapled to a piece of wood. It is useful in getting and maintaining sharp pencil points without constant sharpening. It can be found with pencils and other drawing tools in most art stores.

Pens and Markers

I always find pens and markers to be seductive little toys. Their brightly colored plastic caps catch the light in the store, and one imagines them capable of great things. They're easy to carry around and fun to experiment with. Some are filled with permanent ink; others fade very quickly when exposed to normal light for any length of time. If you find them irresistible, buy a few in a variety of colors. They can be wonderful for journal work, especially for meditative mandalas.

Pastels

There are two types of pastels: oil and chalk. Both are held and applied in the same way as crayons, but they leave a different material on the surface. The chalk pastel leaves a dustlike surface; the oil pastel leaves a surface similar to lipstick used on paper. There is a wider range of quality and composition in pastels than some of the other media we've discussed, because there are numerous types and formulas.

If you are interested in experimenting without investing a great deal of money, you can buy a box of pastels, or you can purchase them individually. Those that sell individually are usually of a higher grade than the boxed set version.

Using expensive, individual oil pastels (especially the French ones) is like drawing with cubes of butter. The experience is very sensuous and is excellent for letting your body create instead of your head. When you feel comfortable with drawing, if you want an interesting and delicious experience, you might buy one excellent pastel in a beautiful color, and just luxuriate in the feel of it.

Brushes

While the quality of brushes is very important to professional artists, in Creative Meditation it is not crucial. Financial considerations forced me originally to buy only two types of brushes, and I find these work for most things; extra brushes and implements can be added as desired.

1. You should have a broad, two- or three-inch flat-edge brush for applying thin washes of color.
2. You should have a #6 pointed brush.

If you use only those two brushes, plus a selection of the materials listed above, you will be adequately prepared for all the projects and exercises listed in this book. This is good news if you plan to do the exercises with a group, because brushes can be very expensive. Eventually, you may want to invest in really good brushes, but let yourself grow into that. Finding a brush that is just right for your personal technique is like finding a comfortable pair of shoes.

Again, let me say that as you progress with this creative discipline, as you return time after time to the art supply land of Oz, you will add your own little touches. You will accumulate new materials, as well as techniques that are uniquely your own.

Glues

When you are doing collage, the type of glue you need will be determined by the weight of materials you're working with and the process you're doing. For instance, if you are attaching stones or shells to the base of your altar, you need a less powerful glue than if you are attaching shells and sand to your hanging self-portrait. Strength, transparency, and adaptability will be the most important characteristics to consider when choosing a glue.

Polymer Medium

Polymer medium is not really a glue, but it works beautifully as a transparent adhesive for lightweight papers, fabrics, and objects. It is amazingly strong. I have mixed sand with it and affixed it to canvas. The sand does not fall off; in fact, if I wanted it off I'd have to scrape it off with a strong, sharp instrument. It's excellent for collage and for incorporating magazine or personal photos into paintings, and it's very versatile.

White Glue

Most white glues have similar properties. You have probably used such a glue in school projects. I don't care for it very much; I suppose this is a personal preference, but it's difficult to apply in a consistent layer, so it creates an uneven collaged surface. This glue can be diluted with water, however, and applied with a brush.

Rubber Cement

Most of you are as familiar with rubber cement as you are with the white glues. I find it a very useful and easy-to-apply adhesive. It's best for simple photo paste-up jobs. It's not very strong, but it is very clean and therefore easy to carry in a mobile art pack. When errant applications dry, rubber cement rubs easily off the surface. You can also use it as a "maskoid," which means that you can apply it to small areas that you want to protect from paint. Instead of having to be very careful with the edges of the painted area, you can make freer brush strokes, removing any dry paint with the rubber cement when you're finished. (A special maskoid can also be purchased for this purpose. It is easier to work with, so if you were going to use this technique often, I'd suggest maskoid rather than rubber cement.)

Paste

I recommend Yes! Paste, which is a versatile and trustworthy adhesive. It can be diluted for use with a brush, or applied very thickly. It is one of the best glues for multipurpose use.

Exercise:
Putting Paint onto a Surface

Let's see now . . . you have your paint, you have a palette, water in containers, brushes, pencils, and rags or paper towels. You're ready to paint!

This part of painting is very simple. Most of the time you want to begin with wet brushes. Put the paint you want to begin with on the palette. Take one brush from the water, and remove the excess water with little strokes of the brush along the side of the water container. Pick up some of the paint with the brush, and take it to the paper. Put it down, and make some kind of a mark.

That is the essence of painting. Honestly. You will simply continue to repeat that act, always returning the brush to the water, then to the paint, then to the paper. Sometimes you'll go from the water to the paper, using the water to manipulate the paint that is already there. Whenever you set down the brush, put it into the water.

You can use the other implements we've talked about on wet or dry paint. You may want to stick things into the paint: pictures, feathers, or pieces of lace, netting, or sand. You can do whatever you want. You have no limitations on this surface. Play, and have fun!

The "Five-Minute-Teaching-Anybody-How-to-Draw-Anything" Guide

HIS IS A little guide to help you create quick images you may need in some of your paintings. It has very little to do with the section in chapter 3 about drawing and seeing, except that it may awaken you to the underlying structure of animals and objects. The goal of this resource is to teach you to see the shapes that make up the whole form of things.

Everything can be created by using basic geometric shapes connected by straight or curved lines. It's very simple once you develop an eye for seeing these shapes. As an example, let's say you want to draw a dream that had in it a horse, a giraffe, and a cat. How would you create a symbolic likeness of these animals?

Here's a horse:

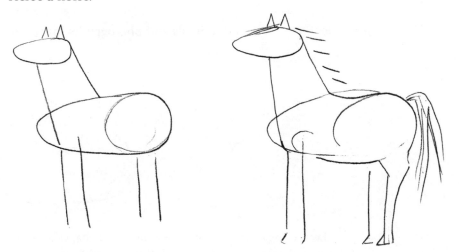

Work in stages using a soft lead pencil and a kneaded eraser.

A giraffe:

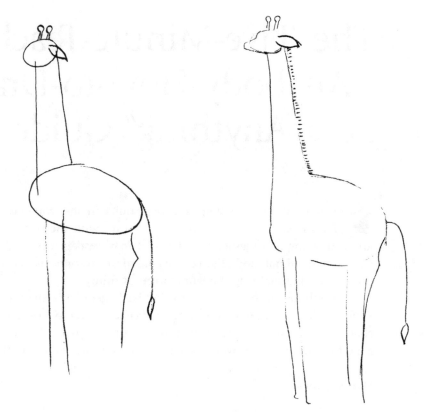

Learn to look closely at real animals and photographs for special features.

A cat:

Everything can be broken down into these shapes for quick symbolic drawings. Circles, ovals, squares, rectangles, and lines: these are the basic vocabulary of image making. When we were children we could draw almost anything, because we could see more simply. The drawings that you do from basic shapes are probably going to resemble those you did in childhood, and you shouldn't let that discourage you. This clarity of vision is something you're striving to regain. Making such simplified drawings is a means toward seeing important structural elements. Often the simplest, most minimal images are the product of profound sight expressed through elegant gesture.

Use books and photographs to study the unique slants and angles that objects have. The head of the giraffe, for instance, is far more complex than a small oval. It will still require you to use your Seeing abilities to put these shapes together.

If you keep practicing—I suggest you do this in your painting journal—you will begin to study the structure of everything around you. Before you know it you'll be seeing the world in a new dimension. You'll come to recognize how much you have assumed and how little you've really known about animals and objects.

If there is one technical tip to keep in mind it's this: practice making ovals and circles with a loose wrist. Tightness in your arm and wrist will restrict you from making the sometimes subtle adjustments in the basic shapes.

Pay special attention to the places and angles where segments meet. For example, where does the neck begin on the back of a horse, and how thick is it? Does it go straight up, or does it carry the head out ahead of the feet? When you begin to look at each segment (of anything) in relationship to the other parts, you will be able to draw things in reasonable likeness.

A human can be created in a number of different ways. Here are some examples, but you'll learn your own style of speaking the language of forms by practicing the vocabulary through your own hand.

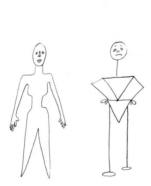

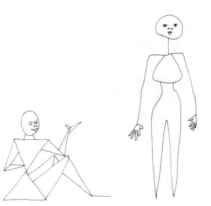

Looking at Pictures

*I*N CHAPTER 3 we talked about the way labeling gets in our way of seeing. The same problem occurs when we look at expressive work. Most of us grow up with a popularized idea of what music is (something melodic), what poetry is (something that rhymes?), what good painting is (something that's pretty!). Now that you are a painter, and you know something about the work that goes into this discipline, you know that becoming a responsible witness to art also requires preparation. Having completed the work suggested in this book, you are probably reevaluating many of the lessons and assumptions you've accumulated over the years. Creating paintings helps us to realize the range of responses possible beyond "I like" and "I don't like." A simple spiritual willingness to receive and be led by the work, coupled with an understanding of some basic elements, can enrich our experience of all art forms.

This resource names and defines in general terms the fundamental elements to look for in your own work, as well as in the works of others. This is given to facilitate the Retrospective exercise in chapter 6, but you can use this as a guideline whenever you take a field trip to a gallery or museum.

This list is based on helping you look first at the work you have done in beginning Creative Meditation. Though we haven't been concerned with the technical elements in painting or drawing, the things we will touch on here are important fundamentals of all art forms. You will, no doubt, develop other criteria as your involvement with the creative process expands, but this resource will give you a starting point for evaluation and appreciation.

What to Look For

Style

"Style" could also be described as "continuity of approach." Each person has a particular feel to her or his work. Look for things such as boldness in strokes or use of color, delicacy of line, or abundant texturing.

Observe and compare the styles of other painters. Pay attention to their use of color, brush strokes, shapes, and images. Use the work of others to ask constructive questions about your own work.

Some people like the style they see emerging in their work, while others don't. If you do not feel good about the style you see, ask yourself what exactly is displeasing. As a tool to gain some distance, imagine that these pieces belong to someone else; try to name the feeling this approach gives you. How would you like to see your work change? Whatever seems distinctive about your work that you do not like can be developed into something new. Try not to judge whether it is good or bad—simply name what you see.

Use of Medium and Materials

Through your growing experience with the media introduced in this book, your knowledge and abilities have grown. Have you developed different ways of applying and using the media? Your early paintings, for instance, may exhibit a tentative approach. Did this change in more recent paintings? Have you experimented with overlays of colors, or various ways of using brushes, sponges, or fingers?

The Retrospective exercise will help you evaluate; if your use of the media is uniform, don't worry about it. Remember that the exercises and projects are here for your continuous use. You can use the instructions as guidelines for many variations in the future.

In observing the work of others, look for unexpected handling. Ask yourself how certain effects might have been achieved. By looking at the works of professionals in galleries, you will discover the properties of media and materials not discussed here. As your own work expands, don't be afraid to experiment with new things. Seek information from art store personnel or other books.

Appreciation requires a discipline of selflessness . . . the expression of personal taste is not our primary goal. The development of taste is: the ability to taste what is present. . . . I am concerned with our power to grasp, to comprehend, to penetrate, and to embrace. . . . The right to opinion must be honored without exception, but not all opinions are equally honorable. Though everyone is free to be who he is, ignorance and cruelty are not freedoms.

M. C. RICHARDS

Line

In the drawing exercises you learned to work exclusively in line. As a third step in evaluating your work, ask yourself how line plays a part in your paintings as well. Look at it as a separate element. Have you developed different types of line through your use of a variety of tools? What tools would you like to experiment with? For example, you might try turning the brush upside down. Incise or scratch lines into wet or dry paint.

Again, make a note to pay attention to the different types of line found in the work of other artists. You might even want to collect examples from magazines and newspapers. Cut them out and paste them into your painting journal. Use these as reference resources for future exploration.

Texture

In spite of the fact that you were not working to develop them, you will have some variety of textures in your work. Chances are you will have the greatest variety of textural qualities in your collage pieces. Look closely at the surfaces you've created. Texture can add an extra dimension to painting. It adds interest and variety without breaking a color scheme, and it can add an emotional tone.

There are many ways of achieving a variety of textures. Papers, objects, or fabric scraps can be glued or sewn onto a surface. You may paint over them or not. Textures can be achieved through visual techniques with marks or drawn patterns.

While tempera paintings on paper cannot be done in heavy or thick layers of paint, since a thick, dried tempera will crack and flake, if you decide to continue to paint with acrylic or oil paint on canvas or canvas board you may want to experiment with impasto technique. Impasto is the art of working with thick amounts of paint that stand up off the canvas surface.

Focus and Balance

Looking at each painting, ask yourself where your eye goes. Is there a definite focus? As you look at the painting, does your gaze drift off the edges of the page? Does the piece have a sense of balance? If you intended to highlight or call attention to one particular focal point, were you able to pull the viewer into that place? Of course, each painting is a bit different. Look for the elements that determine the focus. Color, shape, and line all work together to lead the eye through a composition.

Working Together

*t*HIS RESOURCE IS intended to give support to those who would like to share the experience of Creative Meditation with groups.

Ritual

The inclusion of ritual is one of the most unique characteristics of the Creative Meditation approach to teaching processes of self-expression. Rituals and ceremonies have five important roles in Creative Meditation:

1. A ceremony or ritual is a way of acknowledging the prayerful and spiritual dimensions of the creative process.

2. Ritual provides a foundation for understanding that receptivity and activity are equal parts of self-expression.

3. Beginning the creative process from a spiritual attitude opens the individual to trust and play.

4. Rituals are a way of learning, developing, and celebrating a reverent awareness for the universe, the planet, and all its creatures.

5. Ritual can bring personal healing and deep relaxation, and, when celebrated with others, can be an experience of communion and bonding.

Unfortunately, in most teaching situations rituals are unheard of, except for those little habits that become "ritualistically" done through repetition or mandate (for example, the Pledge of Allegiance, or certain repetitious prayers learned "by heart"). To repeat significant hymns with thoughtless devotion is diametrically opposed to their original purpose of creating impassioned communion through the stirring presence of language or music. When we stop listening to the meaning of our own words, we are left with anemic and meaningless worship.

I don't recommend replacing an existing religious practice with Creative Meditation, nor with the ceremonies that may accompany it. I do, however, encourage people to include more ritualized celebration into their everyday lives as an extension of their existing religious practice. Most of us were taught to take part in the traditional celebrations carried out by others (usually professionally religious figures), so we're unaccustomed to creating our own rituals or ceremonies. Developing such a dimension of our personal practice need not detract from any traditional practices, but it can add to our celebration of the divine and the spiritual dimension of life.

No matter what the size or age of a group, no matter what the occasion, an opening ceremony or ritual establishes the compassionate tone for your work and sets up a sense of anticipation for what is to come.

Rituals and ceremonies can be tremendously important, especially in teaching children. If you anticipate doing Creative Meditation with children, I suggest you assist them in developing their own ceremonies, rather than preplanning and having them follow along. If you lay out a format or outline stating the purpose of each segment, the children can design within that organizational framework.

Closing rituals draw together the members of a group by way of acknowledging their cocreation and reaffirming their mutual support. There's no reason to make celebrations lengthy; in fact, when working with children it's especially important to keep them fairly brief. Affirmation, trust, bonding, and the establishment of sacred space are the essential goals of such a ritual.

For individual work, you may want to establish a regular practice that acknowledges the beginning and ending of your Creative Meditation time, as well as establishing your creative space. Such a practice can be as simple as lighting a candle, ringing a special bell, or playing an instrument (recorders, flutes, ocarinas, drums, and bells are excellent instruments to keep on or near your altar).

Basic Guidelines
for Group Ritual and Ceremony

If you want to expand from private rituals to leading and facilitating others, the following guidelines will be helpful.

1. Work with a partner or small group. Even if you do your creative work alone, you might want to have a group of friends or family members who meet occasionally to share experiences and support. If one person begins as the ritual designer and facilitator, work toward group sharing of these roles. Rituals do not always need to be planned and laid out ahead of time. A group that meets regularly can be spontaneous and develop an opening and closing that fit the mood and needs of the moment.

   If you are asked to lead or facilitate occasional rituals for others (perhaps organizations or clubs), it can be helpful to have a partner to team up with, especially if the group is very large.

2. Always begin by creating a sense of sacred space. Just as with personal work, this can be anything from lighting incense and invoking a moment of silence to actually marking the ritual space with flower petals and ribbons. It does not have to be elaborate, as long as it acknowledges the beginning of a communally creative and prayerful experience.

3. Always have a focus. This can tie in with the theme of the Creative Meditation you will be doing, or with a holiday or occasion.

4. Be environmentally conscious. This is a threefold step. First, evaluate your materials based on ecological considerations (biodegradability, toxicity, recycling potential, etc.). Second, consider the physical limitations of the space in which you are working, and any mobility problems presented to group members. These could be stairs, rocky paths, or sand. Consider lighting and ventilation. Certainly you want to leave any place unmarred by human presence. Third, the environment may provide a focus for your ritual. Beach, forest, desert: each place on the earth offers a million opportunities for celebration.

5. Be inclusive in use of language and participation. This can be very challenging and will require sensitivity and thoughtfulness on the part of any leader. Some people have a great aversion to commonly accepted "God" terminology and socioreligious concepts such as the word *Lord*. If

you think you can read the group along these lines, then trust your judgment about language. If you do not know the group, I suggest using very broad language. The term *Divine Creator,* for example, could be acceptable to a large audience.

Creating ritual can be very educational in this regard. Most important, respect people equally. If you are ever in a situation in which someone comes to you offended by an oversight or terminology, I suggest that you try not to become defensive. Thank them for voicing their feelings, and share your sincere concern about learning some new ways of dealing with the limitations and presumptions of our language as it stands. Usually, when it is understood that you are respectful of individual belief and practices, participants become sympathetic with the challenge to please everyone. A receptive, academic attitude helps to deflect the otherwise personal feelings that such criticism can breed. Tell yourself that you are always open to learning about the beliefs and opinions of others.

Inclusion of participation means that you must also take into account age differences and physical considerations. If you have a very large group, for example, you might want to have simultaneous American Sign Language translation. Remember that dances can be done with hands, and songs can be sung in the dark. Ritual is one more art form that challenges the creativity of the designer.

An essential element to keep in mind is that all participants are equals in a ritual. Those facilitating the ritual must not separate themselves from the activities, nor consider themselves to be more or less important than any other participants. The circle (or oval) is an important nonhierarchical configuration. It allows people to move around easily and keep other participants in view.

6. Have some type of format. Essentially, this means have a beginning, middle, and end. Consider the strengths, needs, and special elements of the group. The most important element for an opening ritual should be a sense of welcoming. Begin your format with something that speaks of hospitality, and then follow with the next important thing you want to establish.

7. Teach songs, dances, and so on before the actual ritual begins. There are four reasons for this:
➤People have a sense of what's coming, and they feel at least somewhat prepared, therefore more relaxed.
➤Learning something together helps people get acquainted.

➤By the time it comes to doing the song or dance, a sense of community will have developed.

➤You won't have to stop the flow of your ritual to interject something new.

8. Facilitate people getting to know each other. I have always had an aversion to the traditional design of theaters and auditoriums, because the seating plan and stage configuration encourage formality and estrangement among audience members. Our bodies respond to such settings with a certain degree of tension and restraint. (I am convinced that this accounts for the presence of bars in opera houses and symphony halls. Alcohol is the compensatory relaxant for the regimentation and stiffness of the environment.)

We teachers have to strive to perfect ourselves in generosity and imagination and the ability to identify ourselves with others.

M. C. RICHARDS

People respond warmly to a welcoming presence. The grace and hospitality of one person can put everyone at ease. Ritual facilitation means developing camaraderie among people. Whether you are working with large groups or small, friends or strangers, this step is equally important. A recognition of common experience and a way of sharing those commonalities usually enhances the relaxation of participants and encourages the commingling of creative energies.

9. Acknowledge the whole experience of life. This is a more subtle guideline. It means that it's important to recognize that ceremonies and rituals are not just for lighthearted celebrations. Sometimes it is important to deal with painful issues; allow the ritual to become a sacred space in which to face and thus transform fears and demons.

10. Give brief and concise explanations as a part of the opening, using clear universal symbols. Symbols that have universal understanding are those connected to the most basic experiences of human existence. A colorful leaf can represent autumn, a collection of shells and sand carry the presence of the ocean. These types of symbols speak a common language that transcends national or linguistic barriers.

Be concise and clear in explaining the agenda and activities you have in mind. Don't assume that participants understand the symbols you've selected. Go over them, explaining their meaning as you intended it.

11. Acknowledge your sources. Whenever resources or reference materials are used, and this includes music and poetry, be sure to credit the source.

12. Include reverential acknowledgment of cosmic elements and ancestors. It is important to understand that ritual is not a superficial tool of Creative Meditation. It is a form of prayer with very ancient roots. Rituals provide a unique opportunity to give thanks to those energies that have brought us here. Through the ceremonial element of Creative Meditation, we take the time to honor the memories of our ancestors—blood relatives, significant historical figures, even members of other species—as well as the ancestral self that we embody.

In keeping with the traditions of indigenous cultures, our gratitude must also be spoken to those elements whose presence we usually take for granted. The ritual is the time to give thanks for water, air, earth, and fire. Creating a sense of sacred space allows a time for the recognition of the beauty and divinity of the planet. It is important to remember that we are made up of these elements, and that in celebrating our universe we also celebrate ourselves with reverence.

In the United States there are no consistent cultural means for teaching children to have reverence for ancestors, other species, or the planet itself. Even the most sincere religious educators seldom place all three of those important aspects of life into the context of their teachings. Yet these are the very basic issues taught by all primal cultures—how has our society lost sight of them? More difficult to answer is, How will we regain that reverence? How and when will we learn to honor and give thanks for each and every element of this mysterious and beautiful universe in which we live? This, of course, was the origin of the custom of saying Grace before meals, a brief moment of prayer as an act of gratitude and remembrance. I suggest that it's time for such prayers whenever we are struck by the blessings of creation. A sunset, a baby, a thunderstorm, a whale: these too are nurturance worthy of praise and gratitude.

Altars

The presence of an altar creates a recognition of sacred space. I find that a designated altar area in a studio or classroom makes an important statement about what is taking place there. If you're working with groups, it isn't necessary to have an altar for every meeting, nor a ritual for every meeting, unless you agree to establish such a tradition. When you do create an altar, there should be some type of ceremony in connection with it. At times you may want to have created the altar in advance, but on other occasions it can be built by the entire group as a part of the ritual.

In the Triptych Altarpiece project in chapter 1, you will find a discussion of what objects can be put on the altar. Certain things are universal and can have a constant presence, while other objects and photos can change according to your own desires. For example, my altar must have candles and some representation of the four elements. I may bring in a clay bowl with some soil in it, a bowl of water, a stick of incense, or some feathers (these symbolize air to me). I always have flowers and some type of colorful fabric (shawls and old curtains from secondhand stores make inexpensive altar cloths). Be careful of candle wax, which can ruin a good altar cloth, and be careful about leaving candles lit when you're not around.

During a ritual, an altar is a good focal point for group energy, and the objects are excellent visual reminders of the ceremonial theme. Within the practice of Creative Meditation, ritual and ceremony maintain the spiritual affirmation of human creativity as sacred blessing.

A Guide to Facilitating Painting and Drawing Experiences

If you have worked with the projects and exercises in this book on your own and feel you'd like to help others discover the Creative Meditation process, the following guidelines will be of some help.

The most important thing for facilitating this approach to creative work is a compassionate and patient spirit. The healing of negative creative self-images is essential to Creative Meditation, and the facilitator of the process must be a trustworthy and compassionate ally.

1. Have firsthand knowledge of all materials. Don't do a project or exercise for the first time as a facilitator. You will feel more confident if you're familiar with all the steps of the exercise as well as all the basic properties of your materials. You will also instill trust in your abilities to teach if you can answer most questions about materials and process. This doesn't mean you have to know everything—just have a comfortable working knowledge of what you're doing.

Begin each project in a new medium with a brief demonstration. Outline the basic properties of the medium, how to use the tools, how to clean up, and where to put things before leaving. (This process is the same for adults and children.) Give only as much technical instruction as you feel will encourage students to venture forward without a fear of "doing it wrong."

At the beginning of this book I suggested that you get to know some-one at your art supply store who would be available to answer your questions. That person may be helpful in answering the questions that come up in group work as well.

2. Do a "check-in" at the beginning of each meeting. This can be a minute of silent personal reflection followed by a sharing of each person's mood or experience of the day. The check-in weaves the energies of individuals together, creating a cohesive group atmosphere. As each person speaks, struggles and triumphs can be shared. The lives we bring to our art are full of stress and criticism, and in a Creative Meditation group we can help each other persevere. The affirmation of others increases our self-trust, making this group environment a hospitable space into which we can relax and express our unique responses to life.

3. Be a constant reminder of the emphasis on process rather than product. Using meditation to set the tone of each meeting is very helpful in this regard.

4. Be available to listen and talk with individuals who are dealing with traumatic memories or other difficulties. Your personal time and encour-agement is tremendously important. Be receptive, and listen closely to the language being used. Without replacing old "shoulds" with new ones, remind each person that they are in a safe space to develop their creative autonomy.

5. Be actively and passively attentive. You must find a balance between being attentive and hovering. Don't hover around people. State clearly that you are available if anyone wants your help, and circulate from time to time. Don't be afraid to make a helpful comment about technique or to suggest a way of expanding something already begun. Give broad opin-ions when you feel they are appropriate.

At times someone will want you to solve a problem for them. Your job is to lead participants to discovery. You can do this by example, or by posing "what if" possibilities. Take part in the project but not through their work. Paint along with everybody else so that they can watch you. Let them know that you are open to questions about your process while you're working.

6. Keep a painting journal, and if you work with people in an ongoing sit-uation, require them to keep one as well. Remember that your personal

creativity is essential to being able to facilitate this process with others. Working and playing in the journal keeps your creative juices flowing and keeps you mentally agile. Anyone who is drawing daily worries much less about mistakes and bad work. Painting journal work, like scale practice for a musician, is the place where you develop skills and technique.

7. Make spiritual practice and ritual inclusive. A Creative Meditation group may have many religious backgrounds. Ceremonies and rituals must be reverential and inclusive of all people. Be mindful of language and sensitive to the needs of the group. The best way to do this is to create rituals together.

8. Keep challenging yourself in your creative process. If you get stuck in a safe place (with certain images, techniques, or processes) push yourself into something new, some endeavor that requires beginner's mind. Such experiences will keep you aware of what your beginning Creative Meditation participants are dealing with.

Exercise:
The Breath of God

This exercise also appears in chapter 1. I include it here as an example of how to stretch the individual exercises to fit group situations. Please refer to the instructions in chapter 1 as a refresher.

To adapt this project for children: Brilliant watercolors are not marked as nontoxic, so don't use straws. This removes the possibility that a child could ingest the watercolors, either by accident or out of curiosity. The medium is sufficiently liquid that children can blow it around on the page without a straw. Also, *do not use bleach with children.*

Supplies

* Paper: Watercolor paper works best, of course, but if your budget does not allow it, an all-purpose drawing paper will work well. Minimum size: fifteen by twenty inches. Don't use newsprint or anything flimsy or very absorbent.
* Straws: I prefer bendable straws.
* Plastic containers of assorted sizes: yogurt, cottage cheese containers, etc., are excellent for this.
* Optional: cotton balls and liquid bleach
* Paper towels

Preparation

Each person should have
* A sheet of paper

* Several containers of pigment (one of each color available). If each person doesn't have his or her own supply of pigments, use the smaller recyclable plastic containers for this.
* One or two empty containers for mixing and diluting
* A container of water: larger, sixteen-ounce cottage cheese container
* A straw
* Paper towels or absorbent rags

How to Proceed for Group Work

Essentially you can follow the directions for individual work. Ask participants to close their eyes to begin, and lead a guided centering and relaxation to music. You may also want to predetermine the break time and introduce the possibility of using bleach to everyone at the same time.

It is best if bleach is not used until several colors have been laid down.

Ask participants to be done about one-half hour before your ending time. At that point, have each person draw a rectangular box in the center on the back of their painting and bring their work into a central circle. They should also bring a pencil with them. (If you have a central altar set up, the work can be laid around the altar.) With the paintings displayed in a circle, play some soft background music and let everyone walk around viewing the exhibit of their work. When they have gone around once, ask them to go around once more, this time more slowly, writing a title on the back of every painting, outside the central box.

Instructions for writing titles: It's easy for these titles to become a jumbled mess, so I suggest you give some instructions to add a little order. The central rectangular box is to be left empty. This is the space that will eventually hold the final title of the painting, which the artist selects from among the possibilities.

Each painting is to be perused individually, turned in every different way until an image emerges. When that image inspires a title, the viewer writes the title along the border of the paper on the back. The title should be legible when the painting is held in the proper direction for that image.

Once all the pieces have been titled by all the participants, they return to their seat with their painting to select a title from those given. If none of the titles feels right, the artist may choose an original title. It's possible that two or even three given titles will come together to create something else.

When everyone has chosen their titles, open a time for sharing the "honorable mention" titles, those that were very good but not quite right. No one is to tell their final title until the end, with everyone standing again in a circle.

This can serve as a ceremonial closure for this creative gathering. (In fact, together with the opening ritual in chapter 2, this can provide a closing ceremony for a workshop or retreat.) As each person individually presents his or her work, they proudly celebrate their creativity with the following declaration:

"This, my own original creation, shall be named: "[Title]."

If you have opened with the Yoruba blessing, the class may respond to the artist with a simple *"Aché,"* which is a Yoruba greeting of affirmation. If you have not done the Yoruba opening blessing, the group can respond ensemble with something like "The universe [or we] welcome(s) your creative gift. Thank you." You might also want to allow time for singing names.

Each project is infinitely adaptable to groups. Let's look at the self-portrait project as an example. A group of people can work simultaneously on this project, coming together for a ceremonial beginning and ending. Work can be done independently. This is an excellent project to bring a family together, or members of a community. If you are having a reunion, for example, you can make art materials available and do the self-portraits as a spontaneous fun event, or ask each person to do one before the gathering. On the day or evening of the reunion, hang the portraits all around the reunion site.

Sing your names (new or old) and acknowledge the fun, courage, and perseverance it took to create the people as well as the images. If you follow the ritual guidelines set up for this project, food can be shared as a closing after each person has introduced his or her self-portrait.

Let your imagination soar with ideas about adapting the individual projects and exercises into group experiences. Some of these would make great additions to parties, while the more contemplative exercises would be appropriate for retreat work. Each group, setting, and occasion will offer new possibilities.

Bibliography

Anthony, Carol. *The Philosophy of the I Ching*. Stow, MA: Anthony Publishing Co., 1981.

Apostolos-Cappadona, Diane. *Art, Creativity and the Sacred: An Anthology in Religion and Art*. New York: Crossroad, 1984.

Arieti, Silvano. *Creativity: The Magic Synthesis*. New York: Harper & Row, 1976.

Ashton, Dore. *Picasso on Art*. New York: Da Capo Press, 1988.

Baruchello, Gianfranco, and John Martin. *Why Duchamp: An Essay on Aesthetic Impact*. New York: Documentext, McPherson & Co., 1985.

———. *How to Imagine: A Narrative on Art, Agriculture, and Creativity*. New York: Bantam, 1985.

Berensohn, Paulus. *Finding One's Way with Clay*. New York: Fireside Books, 1972.

Berger, John. *About Looking*. New York: Pantheon Books, 1980.

Bly, Robert. *News of the Universe: Poems of a Twofold Consciousness*. San Francisco: Sierra Club Books, 1980.

Brueggemann, Walter. *The Prophetic Imagination*. Philadelphia: Fortress Press, 1978.

Chicago, Judy. *Through the Flower: My Struggle as a Woman Artist*. Garden City, NY: Doubleday & Co., 1977.

Chipp, Herschel B., ed. *Resources in Modern Art*. Berkeley: Univ. of California Press, 1968.

Edwards, Betty. *Drawing on the Right Side of the Brain*. Los Angeles: J. P. Tarcher, 1979.

———. *Drawing on the Artist Within*. New York: Fireside Press, 1986.

Eliade, Mircea. *The Sacred and The Profane: The Nature of Religion*. New York: Harcourt Brace Jovanovich, 1959.

Fischl, Eric, and Jerry Saltz. *Sketchbook with Voices*. New York: Alfred van der Marck Editions, 1986.

Flack, Audrey. *Art and Soul: Notes on Creating*. New York: E. P. Dutton, 1986.

Fox, Matthew. *A Spirituality Named Compassion*. Minneapolis: Winston Press, 1979.

———. *Breakthrough: Meister Eckhart's Creation Spirituality*. Garden City, NY: Doubleday & Co., 1980.

———. *Meditations with Meister Eckhart*. Santa Fe, NM: Bear & Co., 1982.

———. *Original Blessing*. Santa Fe, NM: Bear & Co., 1983.

———, ed. *Western Spirituality: Historical Roots, Ecumenical Routes*. Santa Fe, NM: Bear & Co., 1981.

Bibliography

Franck, Frederick. *The Zen of Seeing.* New York: Vintage Books, 1973.

——. *The Awakened Eye.* New York: Vintage Books, 1979.

——. *Art as a Way: A Return to Spiritual Roots.* New York: Crossroad, 1981.

Friend, David. *The Creative Way to Paint.* New York: Watson-Guptill Publications, 1986.

Fromm, Erich. *To Have or To Be?* New York: Harper & Row, 1976.

Gablik, Suzie. *Has Modernism Failed?* New York: Thames & Hudson, 1984.

Gauguin, Paul. *The Writings of a Savage.* Edited by Daniel Guérin. New York: Viking Press, 1978.

Gawain, Shakti. *Creative Visualization.* New York: Bantam, 1985.

Gies, Joseph, and Frances Gies. *Women in the Middle Ages.* New York: Harper & Row, 1978.

Gilot, Françoise. *Matisse and Picasso, A Friendship in Art.* Garden City, NY: Doubleday, 1990.

Gilot, Françoise, and Carlton Lake. *Life With Picasso.* New York: Signet Books, 1965.

Goldwater, R., and M. Treves, eds. *Artists on Art: From the XIV to the XX Century.* New York: Pantheon Books, 1958.

Grosser, Maurice. *The Painter's Eye.* New York: Mentor Books, 1963.

Hagan, Kay Leigh. *Internal Affairs: A Journalkeeping Workbook for Self-Intimacy.* San Francisco: Harper & Row, 1990.

Harman, Willis, and Howard Rheingold. *Higher Creativity: Liberating the Unconscious for Breakthrough Insights.* Los Angeles: J. P. Tarcher, 1984.

Hess, Thomas B., and Elizabeth C. Baker, eds. *Art and Sexual Politics: Why Have There Been No Great Women Artists?* New York: Collier Books, 1974.

Hinz, Evelyn, ed. *Anaïs Nin: A Woman Speaks.* Chicago: Swallow Press, 1975.

Houston, Jean. *The Possible Human.* Los Angeles: J. P. Tarcher, 1982.

Hyde, Lewis. *The Gift.* New York: Vintage Books, 1983.

Janis, Harriet, and Rudi Blesh. *Collage, Personalities, Concepts, Techniques.* Philadelphia: Chilton Books, 1967.

Jopling, Carol F., ed. *Art and Aesthetics in Primitive Societies: A Critical Anthology.* New York: E. P. Dutton & Co., 1971.

Jung, C. G. *The Undiscovered Self.* New York: Mentor Books, 1958.

Jung, C. G., ed., and after his death M. L. von Franz. *Man and His Symbols.* Edited by Marie-Louise von Franz. Garden City, NY: Doubleday & Co., 1964.

Kandinsky, Wassily. *Concerning the Spiritual in Art.* New York: Dover Books, 1977.

Keyes, Margaret Frings. *The Inward Journey: Art and Therapy for You.* Millbrae, CA: Celestial Arts, 1974.

Krishnamurti, J. *Life Ahead.* Wheaton, IL: Theosophical Publishing House, 1963.

Kronenberger, Louis, ed. *Brief Lives: A Biographical Companion to the Arts.* Boston: Little, Brown, 1971.

Lane, John. *The Living Tree: Art and the Sacred.* Hartland, Devon: Green Books, 1988.

Langer, Suzanne K. *Philosophy in a New Key: A Study in the Symbolism of Reason, Rite, and Art.* New York: Harvard Univ. Press, 1951.

——, ed. *Reflections on Art: A Source Book of Writings by Artists, Critics, and Philosophers.* New York: Oxford Univ. Press, 1962.

Lewis, C. S. *The Lion, the Witch, and the Wardrobe.* New York: Macmillan, 1970.

Lippard, Lucy R. *From the Center: Feminist Essays on Women's Art.* New York: E. P. Dutton, 1976.

Lipsey, Roger. *An Art of Our Own: The Spiritual in Twentieth-Century Art.* Boston: Shambhala Publications, 1988.

Lisle, Laurie. *Portrait of an Artist: A Biography of Georgia O'Keeffe.* New York: Washington Square Press, 1980.

London, Peter. *No More Second Hand Art: Awakening the Artist Within.* Boston: Shambhala Books, 1989.

Martland, Thomas R. *Religion as Art: An Interpretation.* Albany, NY: State Univ. of New York Press, 1981.

May, Rollo. *Love and Will.* New York: W. W. Norton, 1969.

——. *The Courage to Create.* New York: W. W. Norton, 1975.

Mayer, Ralph. *The Artists' Handbook.* New York: Viking Press, 1970.

McLuhan, Marshall. *Understanding Media: The Extensions of Man.* New York: Signet Books, 1964.

Miller, Alice. *The Drama of the Gifted Child.* New York: Basic Books, 1981.

Miller, Henry. *Paint What You Like And Die Happy: The Paintings of Henry Miller.* San Francisco: Chronicle Books, 1973.

Milner, Marion [Joanna Field]. *On Not Being Able to Paint.* New York: International Universities Press, 1973.

Munro, Eleanor. *Originals: American Women Artists.* New York: Simon & Schuster, 1979.

Neihardt, John G. *Black Elk Speaks.* New York: Simon & Schuster, 1959.

Neumann, Erich. *Art and the Creative Unconscious.* Princeton, NJ: Princeton Univ. Press, 1959.

Parker, Rozsika, and Griselda Pollock. *Old Mistresses, Women, Art and Ideology.* New York: Pantheon Books, 1981.

Patchen, Kenneth. *What Shall We Do Without Us? The Voice and Vision of Kenneth Patchen.* San Francisco: Sierra Club Books, 1984.

Pfeiffer, John E. *The Creative Explosion: An Inquiry into the Origins of Art and Religion.* Ithaca, NY: Cornell Univ. Press, 1982.

Rank, Otto. *Beyond Psychology.* New York: Dover Publications, 1958.

Rich, Adrienne. *The Dream of a Common Language.* New York: W. W. Norton, 1978.

Richards, M. C. *Centering in Poetry, Pottery and the Person.* Middletown, CT: Wesleyan Press, 1962.

——. *The Crossing Point.* Middletown, CT: Wesleyan Press, 1973.

——. *Toward Wholeness: Rudolph Steiner Education in America.* Middletown, CT: Wesleyan Press, 1980.

Rilke, Rainer Maria. *Selected Poems of Rainer Maria Rilke.* Translated by Robert Bly. New York: Harper & Row, 1981.

——. *Letters to a Young Poet.* New York: Vintage Books, 1984.

——. *Letters on Cezanne.* Edited by Clara Rilke. New York: Fromm International Publishing Corp., 1985.

Robbins, Lois. *Waking Up in the Age of Creativity.* Santa Fe, NM: Bear & Co., 1985.

Rogers, Carl. *On Becoming a Person.* Boston: Houghton Mifflin, 1961.

Rogers, Peter. *A Painter's Quest: Art as a Way of Revelation.* Santa Fe, NM: Bear & Co., 1987.

Rothenberg, M.D., Albert. *The Emerging Goddess: The Creative Process in Art, Science and Other Fields.* Chicago: Univ. of Chicago Press, 1982.

Saitzyk, Steven L. *Art Hardware: The Definitive Guide to Artists' Materials.* New York: Watson-Guptill Publications, 1987.

Samuels, Mike, and Nancy Samuels. *Seeing with the Mind's Eye: The History, Techniques, and Uses of Visualization.* New York: Random House, 1986.

Schmied, Weiland. *Tobey.* New York: Harry N. Abrams.

Snyder-Ott, Joelynn. *Women in Art.* Millbrae, CA: Les Femmes Publishing, 1978.

Spector, Jack J. *The Aesthetics of Freud: A Study in Psychoanalysis and Art.* New York: McGraw-Hill, 1974.

Starhawk. *The Spiral Dance.* San Francisco: Harper & Row, 1979.

———. *Dreaming the Dark.* San Francisco: Harper & Row, 1982.

———. *Truth or Dare.* San Francisco: Harper & Row, 1987.

Swimme, Brian. *The Universe Is a Green Dragon.* Santa Fe, NM: Bear & Co., 1984.

Sylvester, David. *The Brutality of Fact: Interviews with Francis Bacon.* New York: Thames & Hudson, 1987.

Taylor, Jeremy. *Dream Work: Techniques for Discovering the Creative Power in Dreams.* Ramsey, NJ: Paulist Press, 1983.

Teish, Luisah. *Jambalaya: The Natural Woman's Book of Personal Charms and Spells.* San Francisco: Harper & Row, 1985.

Teresa of Avila. *The Interior Castle.* Ramsey, NJ: Paulist Press, 1979.

Thomas, Dylan. *The Poems of Dylan Thomas.* Edited and with an introduction and notes by Daniel Jones. New York: New Directions, 1971.

Trungpa, Chögyam. *Shambhala: The Sacred Path of the Warrior.* New York: Bantam, 1986.

Ueland, Brenda. *If You Want to Write: A Book about Art, Independence and Spirit.* St. Paul, MN: Graywolf Press, 1938.

Uhlein, Gabriele. *Meditations with Hildegard of Bingen.* Santa Fe, NM: Bear & Co., 1982.

von Franz, Marie-Louise. *Active Imagination: Encounters with the Soul.* Santa Monica, CA: Sigo Press, 1981.

Walker, Alice. *The Color Purple.* New York: Washington Square Press, 1982.

Watts, Alan W. *The Way of Zen.* New York: Vintage Books, 1957.

Welwood, John, ed. *Challenge of the Heart: Love, Sex, and Intimacy in Changing Times.* Boston: Shambhala Publications, 1985.

Williams, Tennessee. *Three by Tennessee.* New York: Signet Classics, 1976.

Zinker, Joseph. *Creative Process in Gestalt Therapy.* New York: Vintage Books, 1978.

Index

For information concerning lectures, workshops, trainings,
or consultations please write to Adriana Diaz,
P.O. Box 27423, Oakland, CA 94602.